Murder In Wisconsin

Most Evil Serial Killers in Wisconsin History

Written by
Jack Rosewood
&
Dwayne Walker

Copyright © 2015 by Wiq Media

ALL RIGHTS RESERVED

No part of this book may be reproduced, stored in a retrieval system, or transmitted in any form or by any means, electronic, mechanical, photocopying, recording, scanning, or otherwise, without the prior written permission of the publisher.

ISBN-13: 978-1519411563

Table of Contents

Introduction 1

Ed Gein 3

The monster of Plainfield 3

Chapter 1: Did his mother make him do it? 5

A twisted love 6

School years paint bleak picture 8

First death changes family dynamics 8

Fire at the farm 9

Mother's death changes everything 10

Chapter 2: Taking cemetery visits just a little too far 12

When corpses lose their charm 14

Bernice Worden: An infamous death 16

Chapter 3: Stepping into a house of horror 17

Walking into hell 18

Worden's death reveals a macabre house of horrors ..20

Unintended rage has consequences 22

Chapter 4: A psychiatric gold mine 24

State takes over 25

Story of the year 26

Sane or insane? Experts ponder the question..............27

Adeline Watkins: A sad spinster craving the spotlight..28

Aftermath 30

Back to court, 10 years later..31

Gein: The later years 33

A never ending trail of visitors.....................................35

A child remembers 36

Notable inspirations..37

David Spanbauer 39

A monster becomes a remorseless killer 39

Chapter 1: Spanbauer was born for bigger crimes 41

Living the straight and narrow? Hardly........................43

Next rape results in slap on the wrist 44

Chapter 2: Released after 12-year prison stint...............46

Laurie Depies: Gone in the night 47

A 10-year-old girl on a bike 48

A predator can't stop hunting 50

Chapter 3: Cora Jones, A bike marks the spot 52

Fear or premonition? 53

Volunteers come in droves 54

A legacy left in words 55

Chapter 4: Mistakes lead to arrest 57

Attempted robbery seals Spanbauer's fate 58

Photo brings ruse crumbling down 59

In time, a confession comes 60

Confessing reveals truth for families 60

Arrest brings back bad memories 63

Chapter 5: No final trial for David Spanbauer 65

Tell-all falls through 67

No tears for Spanbauer 68

Chapter 6: The aftermath 70

A killer confesses 71

Jeffrey Dahmer 73

Milwaukee cannibal searches for a friend 73

Chapter 1: Birth of an obsession 75

Hormones and horror 76

Drinking doesn't diminish sick fantasies 78

Chapter 2: Dahmer turns fantasy to reality 80

The aftermath of a murder 81

Chapter 3: Second victim opens the floodgates 84

Trouble at grandma's house 85

Killing was a means to an end 86

Things begin to escalate 87

Dahmer begins saving trophies 89

A close call 90

Prison term temporarily protects young men 91

Time away makes Dahmer ravenous 92

Hunger escalates 93

Real-life skeletons in the closet 94

Ill-fated shopping trip 95

Gay advocate's voice silenced 97

A brush with necrophilia 97

An unlikely victim 98

Police make a deadly mistake 99

Apartment of death 102

If at first you don't succeed... 103

Was probation officer to blame? 105

Another tasty victim 106

Dahmer's final victim 107

Tracy Edwards ends Dahmer's fantasy 108

Surprises in store 109

Chapter 3: Dahmer's house of horrors revealed 111

Father's support never wavers.................................... 112

Steven Hicks found 113

A cannibal or a madman? 114

Evaluating madness 114

Chapter 5: The trial of Jeffrey Dahmer............................ 118

Insanity plea hard card to play 121

A madman in disguise 121

Chapter 6: The aftermath 124

A sandwich still causes nightmares 125

Did Dahmer kill Adam Walsh?..................................... 126

Walter Ellis 128

DNA mistakes almost let him get away 128

Chapter 1: DNA mistakes slow arrest 130

Police downplay mistakes 131

Not who he seemed 131

Chapter 2: Victim list spans 20 years 133

One day later, a second victim dies 134

Just like so much trash 134

DNA match not enough for arrest 135

Abandoned 136

Hiding behind a new M.O. 138

Too close for comfort? 138

Another prostitute chooses wrong mark 140

Making sure to leave evidence behind 141

Chapter 3: Trial a farce for victims' families 143

Conclusion 146

A Note From The Author 154

Introduction

There's something about a Wisconsin winter, perhaps, that drives people a little bit mad.

The snows start as early as October and sometimes don't end until late April. During the worst of the months - the grey, gloomy days of January and February - frigid temperatures dip well below zero and feel especially harsh when accompanied by the bone-chilling winds that sweep off of lakes Michigan and Superior.

It's a place suitable only for the very resilient, and some never know if the long winters will turn them into real-life versions of Stephen King's Jack Torrance from "The Shining." At least not until it is too late.

Home to hip college cities and quiet mill towns along the Wisconsin River, Wisconsin is a dichotomy of sorts, part bucolic rolling hills dotted with farm fields, part thick Northwoods pine forest, where mobster Al Capone built a stone hideout where he would go when things in Chicago got sticky.

Hunting is a popular sport, although as we all know, some hunters aren't so much on the prowl for deer or quail as they are for victims.

Given the terminally gray skies that seemingly last forever – broken only by a few short months of spring, summer and fall - it's no surprise that the state has the dubious honor of being home to some of the most depraved serial killers of all time, including one of the first and most notorious, Ed Gein.

One could say it was the cold, the snow drifts, the ice and the gray skies. And maybe they'd be right. Maybe.

Ed Gein

The monster of Plainfield

Residents of Plainfield still don't like to talk about the heinous crimes of loner handyman Eddie Gein, even though it has been decades since police found hardware store owner Bernice Worden gutted like a deer and hanging headless in Gein's dilapidated woodshed.

For that small Wisconsin town, the media circus that followed Gein's arrest, clogging streets and backing up traffic, brought too much attention, and once the rabid reporters and their cameras with smoking flashes were gone, Plainfield residents only wanted to get back to the business of living their lives.

But normal would prove to be terribly tricky, given the sheer horror of what police found in Gein's house when they searched the home, their passage initially illuminated only by flashlight. Inside, authorities learned that Gein had decorated his clapboard farmhouse with chairs and a lampshade crudely upholstered with human skin, the faces of human heads stuffed with newspaper and a woman's lips adorning the drawstring on a window shade, among numerous other nightmare-inspiring items.

In his kitchen were human skulls that he used for soup bowls, a scenario so macabre and awful that Wisconsinites made up a few jokes - ("What did Ed Gein give his girlfriend for Valentine's Day? A box of farmer fannies," and "What did Ed Gein say to the sheriff who arrested him? Have a heart.") - in order to cope with the sheer horror of their neighbor's crimes.

But soon enough, the reality of Gein's depravity slowly sinking in and the jokes known as Geiners stopped, as did any talk about Gein and his crimes by Plainfield residents.

After all, there was nothing funny about the vest crafted from a female torso that Gein liked to wear outside to dance under the moonlight, nor the shoebox full of female vulvas gathered from corpses he'd dug up from their graves that were also among the grisly finds that police discovered on that chilly day in November of 1957.

Instead, the depravity of it all would leave a nation reeling, and Plainfield wondering what could have happened to make Ed Gein go off the rails and descend so far into the depths of hell.

CHAPTER 1:
Did his mother make him do it?

Edward Theodore Gein, born in August of 1906 in La Crosse, Wisconsin, had a mother from which nightmares are made.

Devoutly religious, Augusta Gein's sharp tongue – no doubt Stephen King had in mind Augusta Gein when he created the fanatically religious and cruel mother in Stephen King's "Carrie," who drove her daughter to kill - sent Ed's alcoholic father George deeper into the bottle while giving Ed and his older brother Henry some seriously distorted ideas about women.

As far as Augusta was concerned, women aside from herself were the spawn of Satan, little more than trollops with a mission to ruin men's lives, and she did everything in her power to protect her boys from their painted and perfumed clutches.

Augusta ruled their home with a puritanical, domineering hand, but still, Ed worshipped the woman who ran the family grocery store almost single-handedly while George grew drunker and more abusive, until the city of La Crosse, nestled along the banks of the Mississippi River, became steeped in what she saw as too much sin, forcing her to sell the store in 1914 and move to the sanctuary that would be Plainfield.

A twisted love

But Plainfield would prove to be a sanctuary for none of them. Augusta watched her husband descend into the depths of his bottle, becoming angrier, more abusive and less able to provide anything for his family, and she grew to hate the man intensely.

Eddie, meanwhile, so adored his mother that psychiatric experts later said he had a bit of an Oedipus complex when it came to his feelings about Augusta, who was, to hear her tell it, the only good woman left in Wisconsin.

"My mother was a saint," Ed later told anyone who would listen.

But his own views were likely twisted by her very rigid ideals.

"Young children are like sponges and it is likely that Ed absorbed everything his mother conveyed to him through her strict religious code," one psychologist said. "By isolating her children from the outside world, Ed was given the message that the world was a dangerous place and she was protecting him from it. This would have acted to exacerbate

Ed's image of her as a 'saint.' Young children do not tend to question what their caregivers do or say, but accept that what they are doing is within their best interest."

Still, the dichotomy of Augusta's stringent belief system alongside Ed's growing sexual desires created a conflict inside him that would simmer for years.

According to one report, when he was 12, his mother caught Ed masturbating in the bath. The woman instantly reacted by squeezing his genitals, calling them "the curse of men."

Of course he was tormented.

"It is possible that Ed developed an angelic perception of his mother in order to cope with the abuse," one psychologist said. "There is also some evidence that Augusta brainwashed Ed through frequently claiming that all women, with the exception of herself, were evil. The bond Ed developed with his mother as a child literally controlled the rest of his life, with his home becoming a shrine to her."

Augusta kept her boys close to home, and once in Plainfield, they went to school, then came home and worked the 195-acre farm. Augusta discouraged friendships, so her boys rarely left for anything other than a few side jobs for neighbors.

School years paint bleak picture

The boys attended Roche-a-Cri grade school, a one-room schoolhouse with 12 students. Ed was average at school, but an excellent reader. Still, he was shy, sensitive and effeminate, which made him a target for bullies. Ed was shunned and teased by the other kids, in part because of a lazy eye, but also because he had a lesion on his tongue that impacted his speech.

Given his handicaps, he didn't make friends easily, which was just as well, since any attempts at friendship were met by severe abuse at the hand of his mother, who took every opportunity to berate her boys into submission for fear they would end up just like their father.

As for George, when Ed came home crying from the torment he suffered at school, he received no sympathy from him. Instead of comfort, Gein was met with a drunken beating.

No matter where he was, there was clearly no escape for young Eddie.

First death changes family dynamics

When father George died of a heart attack in 1940, life grew even more constricted for Ed and Henry, both of whom still lived on the farm. They did odd jobs around town to help support their mother, but she kept close tabs on her sons.

For his part, in addition to handyman-type labor, Ed sometimes took babysitting jobs, which suited him well since he got along better with children than he did with adults.

Augusta, meanwhile, continued her barrage of warnings, so much so that younger brother Henry started to reject her fanatical ideals, and grew somewhat critical of Ed's abnormal attachment to their mother.

Ed couldn't have been pleased.

Fire at the farm

A few years later, on May 16, 1944, a brush fire threatened the family farm, and both brothers headed out to fight the blaze.

They each approached from different directions, and by nightfall, the fire was out. Henry, however, was missing.

Police were called, and in a move that would cast suspicion on him until he died, Ed led them directly to his brother, who was lying dead in the brush, a bruise on his forehead. He was untouched by fire.

"Funny how that works," said Ed.

Sure, police — and neighbors — had their suspicions, but there was nothing linking Henry's bruises to Ed, and nothing was pursued.

Henry's death was ruled asphyxiation. But from his grave, it's possible he was thinking that perhaps he shouldn't have been so critical of Ed's diehard devotion to their mother.

Mother's death changes everything

A little more than a year after Henry's death, Augusta Gein suffered a series of debilitating strokes, and died just a few days after Christmas, on December 29, 1945.

Eddie, who had done everything his mother ever asked of him, was devastated, and he immediately turned much of the farmhouse into a shrine to Augusta, cordoning off her bedroom and other rooms, leaving only the kitchen and a small room off the kitchen that he used as a bedroom, for himself. It would be these rooms that he would soon be decorating to his liking.

Within a year, neighbors began complaining about Ed's smell. Without his mother to nag him into bathing, he tended to skip hygiene and laundry altogether.

While he continued to do odd jobs around town – including babysitting for neighbors' children - he spent his spare time reading, and developed a particular fondness for stories about tribal head shrinking, cannibalism and other exotic oddities.

And it was now, perhaps triggered by his mother's death combined with abject loneliness, or maybe finally free to express his true self, that Ed slowly transformed from odd man to monster.

CHAPTER 2:
Taking cemetery visits just a little too far

He spent a lot of time at the cemetery, visiting his mother, until eventually he enlisted the help of a mentally disabled friend named Gus to help him dig up her body. Gein immediately twisted off her head, and used techniques he had learned in his beloved books to preserve it.

That first treasure eventually proved to be not enough for Gein, who soon developed a particular fondness for the Obituary section of the newspaper.

When women who resembled his mother in any way passed away – he favored middle aged women with larger, more generously padded builds - he would call on his friend Gus to help him dig up the bodies. He then harvested an array of body parts, especially so the outer layer of skin, which he would peel off and wear to give himself the illusion of having breasts and a vagina, to add to his gruesome collection.

Gein would later tell police he wore the skin because he wanted to know what it felt like to be a woman, a confession that suggested he might have been transgender.

Unfortunately for Gein, while his grave robberies occurred about the same time Christine Jorgensen was making headlines for coming home from Denmark as one of the first known male-to-female sex reassignment surgeries, the man just didn't have the New York-born Jorgensen's elegance or class. He was a grizzled Midwestern hunter and farmer who favored flannel caps and overalls, and would never have been in a position to make his dream of being a woman – if at all true – a reality.

It is more likely that Gein – like the character of Norman Bates in "Psycho" who was inspired by him – wore the grisly pieces as a way to keep his mother alive, especially because he tended to choose women who fit his mother's description when perusing the obituaries for victims.

Or perhaps it was a bit of both.

"Ed was less interested in the female body and more interested in reclaiming his mother," one psychologist said. "The female body reminded him of his mother and the ultimate reminder of her would be to have a sex change."

Dr. R. Warmington, one of the first psychiatrists to interview Gein after his arrest, said that Ed's "motivation is elusive and uncertain but several factors come to mind – hostility, sex, and a desire for a substitute mother in the form of a replica or body that could be kept indefinitely."

He might have been satisfied with corpses, if Gus hadn't gone to live in an old folks' home, leaving Ed on his own, an impossible position for successful grave robbing, which was no one-man job.

Since his proclivity for collecting female body parts hadn't waned, Gein had a problem, and murder was the only answer.

When corpses lose their charm

A native of Chicago, bar owner Mary Hogan was a large woman, about 5'8" and 200 pounds, the right size to grapple with unruly drunks and win.

Twice divorced, she ran her Bancroft establishment — located about six miles from the farmhouse of Ed Gein - for five years, before she went missing on Dec. 8, 1954, at about 4:30 p.m. The bar was empty — her afternoon customers had already staggered home — and she likely would have locked up before making herself some supper in her adjoining living quarters.

When the tavern didn't open the next day, patrons alerted Portage County sheriff Harold Thompson, who broke into the place, only to find a puddle of blood on the floor and a spent shell casing from a .32 rifle.

There were no clues, no witnesses and no theories about what might have happened to Hogan, and the idea of murder didn't even cross the sheriff's mind. It didn't cross anyone's mind, really, despite the blood.

Even Elmo Ueeck, who was working with Ed the day after Mary Hogan's murder. Ed told Elmo that he had killed Mary Hogan and had hung her at his house. Elmo didn't believe him.

"If you'd spent more time courting Mary Hogan, she'd be cooking for you instead of being missing," said one of Ed's neighbors, to which Eddie responded with a smile, "She's not missing. She's down at the house now."

It turned out, however, that Sheriff Thompson was a bit derelict in his duties. About a year after Hogan went missing, the tavern was reopened by Mr. and Mrs. Hank Sherman, who reportedly found a few clues, including a man's cap that appeared to be stained with something that appeared to be blood, in the living quarters formerly occupied by Mary Hogan.

How were they to know that Gein had shot Hogan and then dragged her body home on a sled, turning her face into a macabre work of art that he'd hung on his wall?

From time to time, people did notice Gein's odd artwork, but he was able to convince them that the trophies he'd harvested from corpses were really nothing more than wartime souvenirs his cousin had brought back after fighting the Japanese in the Pacific during World War II.

Bernice Worden: An infamous death

It would be three years before Ed Gein again felt the urge to gather more body parts, and unlucky for her, it was Bernice Worden, who ran Plainfield's corner hardware store, who would catch his fancy.

The day before he killed her, Ed had stopped at the hardware store, asked about the price of antifreeze, then chatted a while with the 58-year-old woman's son Frank, about hunting season, which started the next day.

He told both that he would be back by the next day.

But when Frank returned from hunting on November 17, 1957, he was concerned when he saw that not only was his mother not at her usual spot behind the counter, but the back door of the store was wide open.

When he went inside, he found a trail of blood leading from the front of the store to the open back door, along with the last receipt his mother had written.

It was for a half-gallon of antifreeze.

CHAPTER 3:
Stepping into a house of horror

Gein was found eating supper at his neighbor Lester Hill's house, and was promptly arrested.

From the back of the police car, as Deputy Dan Chase questioned him, Gein said, "Somebody framed me."

"Framed you for what?" asked Chase.

"Well, Mrs. Worden," responded Eddie.

"What about Mrs. Worden?" asked Chase, who hadn't yet mentioned why Gein was sitting in the back of the cop car.

"Well, she's dead, ain't she?" Gein replied.

"How do you know she's dead?" the officer asked from the driver's seat.

Gein attempted to tell Chase that the Hills had been talking about it during supper – "Well, they were talking about it in there," he said – but unless they had seen Bernice Worden's body earlier and failed to call police, that was impossible.

With Gein in custody, the sheriff and other authorities headed to Gein's farmhouse to look for evidence. Nothing could have prepared them for what they would find.

Walking into hell

When Arthur Schley felt something brush against his shoulder after he entered Ed Gein's summer kitchen, which doubled as a woodshed, he didn't think much of it, until he shined his flashlight on what would turn out to be Bernice Worden's headless body, gutted like a deer.

He promptly ran outside to throw up, which has to be excused, given that at the time, most of the area's officers were regular people with regular day jobs who had volunteered to serve as deputies on a part-time basis. They were hardly prepared for something like this.

"The body had been cleaned and handled in a way similar to that used in a slaughterhouse," officer Earl Kileen said, adding later – after Worden's heart was found in Ed's kitchen, stuffed into a sack in front of Gein's potbellied stove - that "it appears to be cannibalism."

The cannibalism statement "sent dozens of people to their doctors suffering from stomach problems after remembering eating packages of 'venison' given to them by Gein," according to reports.

But despite the horrific finds in the house, including Worden's head in a burlap sack, her ears pierced with nails and tied with twine, as though it had already been prepared to become art for Eddie's walls, a belt made of nipples, a table with human bones for legs, cannibalism wasn't part of Ed's repertoire.

Of course, that didn't make the house – which appeared to be a hoarder's house in the rooms where Ed lived, but was otherwise pristine in the rooms he had sealed off, aside from some dust – any less macabre.

"My first impression was some degree of shock," remembered Allen Wilimovsky of the state crime lab, which was called as soon as the first dismembered body part was discovered. "I momentarily stepped back and without saying anything other than thinking to myself, 'What type of individual would do something like this?'"

While flashlights were at first the only light officers had to search by, they soon employed spotlights, given the gruesome finds tucked in dark corners, including the box of vulvas, one fresh and doused in salt, excised in rectangular sections removed with fine attention to detail, the dried face and hair of Mary Hogan, carefully peeled from her skull, hanging in a bag on the back of a door, four noses in a jar.

"I've been killing for seven years," said Gein on the night of his arrest, even as he said that Bernice Worden's shooting was a complete accident, occurring when the loaded Marlin rifle he was looking at accidentally discharged, striking Mrs. Worden.

Worden's death reveals a macabre house of horrors

It's no wonder that Plainfield sheriff Arthur Schley almost mucked up the works when he got a little physical while interrogating Gein, and slammed the farmer against the jail wall in an attempt to get him to confess to killing Bernice Worden, whose cash register was found amid Gein's macabre collection.

Schley had just spent the night touring Gein's house of horrors, and had not only seen Bernice Worden's headless body hanging from the rafters of Gein's shed, but also her head, tucked into a burlap sack with nails through her ears tied together with twine, apparently in preparation for hanging on the wall.

It was, Schley said, "just too horrible. Horrible beyond belief."

It was not enough to get a confession, however.

"In spite of the third degree treatment, Gein did not confess that night," wrote Judge Robert Gollmar in his 1984 book, "Ed Gein."

What he did say, however, was that he was a bit confused and his memory was fuzzy.

He told Kileen that he indeed went to Bernice Worden's store with a glass jug to order some antifreeze.

"Mrs. Worden said, 'Do you want a gallon of antifreeze?' 'No,' I said, 'Only a half-gallon.' I held the glass jug for her while she poured the anti-freeze into it. It was 99 cents. I gave her a dollar, and got one cent change.

"I don't know what happened then. She glanced out the window and said, 'they are checking deer out there.'"

Then, his memory becomes vague.

"I do remember dragging her across the floor. I remember loading her body into the truck."

Gein was referring to the hardware store delivery truck, which was missing when Worden's son Frank arrived at the store. It was usually parked behind the store.

"Then I drove the truck into the pine trees and walked back to town. And I got my car and drove it out there and loaded her body into the back of the car. Then I drove out to my farm and took the body out of the car and hung it up by its heels in the woodshed. I thought I was dressing out a deer. It's the only explanation that comes to my mind."

Gein was then asked if he had killed anyone else, and he said, "Not to my knowledge."

Unintended rage has consequences

Schley's momentary lapse of self-control, which some later said led to Gein's head slamming against the concrete wall - would have consequences, however.

Anything Gein said that night, even though it offered little by way of real evidence, but suggested an understanding that he needed to hide the crime, become inadmissible in court.

"Later, because of this occurrence in the jail and the testimony of psychiatrists, I suppressed the confession Gein made to Joe Wilimovsky of the Wisconsin crime lab. That Sheriff Schley's conduct was greatly regretted by Schley himself was established by many of his acquaintances," said the judge. "Shortly before Gein's trial in 1968, Schley died of a heart attack. There were those in Waushara County who believed that worry over his being subpoenaed to testify hastened his death."

Gein confessed to digging up graves, and a week or so later officers exhumed two caskets to determine the truth of the confession. They found the graves of both Mrs. Eleanor Adams and Mrs. Mabel Everson, buried in 1951, were empty.

Horrified at the thought of discovering more empty graves, police stopped digging.

Over the next week, officials were able to determine that the remains of at least 15 people were scattered throughout Gein's property, including in his home, in his trash heap and in the ash pit where he burned garbage.

And if Plainfield had hopes of keeping things quiet, both Time and Life ran features on the Ed Gein story, likely inspired by Waushara County District Attorney Earl Kileen's initial words to reporters, hinting that Gein had consumed parts of the dead.

Add necrophilia to the mix, and reporters – as well as their rabid readers – were beside themselves.

And while Gein sometimes masturbated with the vulvas he cut from the corpses, he never had sex with the dead, he said – in fact, Gein's sex life was limited exclusively to masturbation, and he had fulfilled his mother's desire that he remain a virgin, untouched by female flesh.

He did not, Gein said, because "they smelled too bad."

CHAPTER 4:
A psychiatric gold mine

Ed was taken before a judge, technically being charged with robbery. Authorities saved the murder charges born from Bernice Worden's death, and waited for a determination of Gein's sanity.

That is something that would never come.

On November 23, 1957, a psychologist and psychiatrist who interview Ed called him schizophrenic and said he was a "sexual psychopath."

One psychologist might have fed Gein some memories, based on the following interaction during the evaluations to determine his sanity.

Q. "Do you have any recollection, Eddie, of taking any of those female parts, the vagina specifically, and holding it over your penis to cover the penis?"

A. "I believe that's true."

Q. "You recall doing that with the vaginas of the bodies of other women?"

A. "That I believe I do remember; that's right."

Q. "Would you ever put on a pair of women's panties over your body and then put some of these vaginas over your penis?"

A. "That could be."

Other reports say that Ed would take the excised female genitals and place them inside a pair of panties that he would then wear, giving him the illusion of femininity.

State takes over

Two days later – on Nov. 25, 1957, the state took over the Gein case, especially given the speculation that Gein had driven out of the county in order to procure new corpses, along with the knowledge that Mary Hogan, whose Bancroft tavern was in nearby Portage County, was also killed outside Waushara County.

"Developments in the case now indicate a statewide concern in ascertaining all the facts," said Governor Thompson. "Certainly the investigation should exhaust the possibilities of additional homicides being committed."

On December 12, 1957, Ed Gein was interviewed by Dr. Edward Schubert, a psychiatrist at Waupun's Central State Hospital, who found that Ed had an "abnormally magnified attachment to his mother."

Schubert sent the judge a packet declaring Gein insane, and suggested that Gein be permanently committed to the hospital. It would be the case of Schubert's life, and he would be remembered for Gein as much as any other player in the sick, sad story. The judge received it on December 17, 1958, a few weeks before the sanity hearing was scheduled to begin.

Story of the year

At end of the year, only a few weeks after Gein's house of horrors was discovered, his story was named the top in the state according to an Associated Press poll - ahead of the Braves winning the world championship, Sen. McCarthy dying, William Proxmire being elected senator, Mark Catlin Jr. fined for unethical conduct as an attorney, eight children dying in a Park Falls home fire, Kohler Co. found to have unfair labor practices, ex-sheriff Michael Lombardi of Waushara County charged with misconduct in office, state traffic deaths setting a record as the third highest in history, and a $2 million fire that ravaged the business district of Reedsburg.

Apparently, 1957 was also the first year Wisconsin employed daylight savings time, and that story didn't make the list at all. The new stadium for the Green Bay Packers was also a contender, but failed to place.

Sane or insane? Experts ponder the question

At Gein's sanity hearing, on January 6, 1958, all the evidence was brought to the Waushara County Courthouse, and psychiatrists discussed what they had learned about Gein during extensive interviews.

According to Shubert, a psychiatrist at Central State Hospital for the Criminally Insane, Gein was hoping to bring the dead back to life through sheer will – again in hopes of provoking the return of his mother – and his failure left him despondent.

"There is ample reason to believe that his violation of the graves was in response to the demands of his fantasy life, which was motivated by his abnormally magnified attachment to his mother," Shubert said.

Experts debated Bernice Worden's gruesome death, the preserved skin, the belt of nipples, Gein's suit of female body parts that he wore around the house, the skull bowls, the chair and lamps crudely upholstered in skin, bits of fat still hanging from them, the skulls that replaced bedposts, the shoebox full of excised female genitalia, the faces stuffed with newspaper and hung on the wall like hunting trophies.

Gein himself talked about his actions, including his grave robbing, and said that most of it happened in a fugue state of sorts.

"Once, when I was digging, I came out of the daze," he said. He immediately put down the shovel and went home.

Waushara County Circuit Court Judge Robert Bunde found Gein to be chronically mentally ill, and best off sent to Waupun's Central State Hospital, a facility where he could be supervised for the rest of his life.

He was sentenced to Central State for an undetermined amount of time, which kept the door open for Gein to someday be tried for the murder of Bernice Worden, if he had sufficiently recovered.

Adeline Watkins: A sad spinster craving the spotlight

Ed Gein's mother had made clear to her son that women were the epitome of all evil, Satan with soft skin, and Gein never dated.

Still, that didn't stop one woman from making national news by reporting that she had dated Gein for 20 years, and that he'd even proposed.

The story, clearly false, appeared in the Minneapolis Tribune, and was picked up by other news outlets, likely eager to cash in on a new angle to the Gein story.

According to Watkins, it was on Feb. 6, 1955, when Gein allegedly asked her for her hand – "not in so many words, but I knew what he meant," she told the newspaper, "I turned him down. Not because there was anything wrong with him. There was something wrong with me, I guess. I was afraid I wouldn't be able to live up to what he expected of me."

(If Gein's "expectations" involved living in his depravity-filled house, she was likely right.)

Watkins, who described Gein as "sweet and kind," said the two talked about books – Gein favored stories about exotic places like Africa and Asia – and murder.

"I guess we discussed every murder we had ever heard about," she said. "Eddie told how the murderer did wrong, what mistakes he had made. I thought it was interesting."

They also sometimes frequented the many bars between Plainfield and Wisconsin Rapids.

"I liked to drink beer sometimes," Watkins said, "but I would almost have to drag Eddie into a tavern. He would much rather have gone to a drugstore for a milk shake."

How sad that a seemingly normal woman would use the gruesome crimes of a sick old man to garner her 15 minutes of fame?

Aftermath

On March 20, 1958, Gein's dilapidated white farmhouse mysteriously burned to the ground, ending plans for an auction that would have again turned Plainfield into a circus of curiosity seekers eager to purchase a piece of America's most nightmare-inducing crimes.

"Just as well," said Gein when learned of the news.

But some items survived, and that same year, Gein's 1949 Ford sedan with whitewall tires was purchased for $760 by Bunny Gibbons, a Rockford, Illinois, man who made his living as a carnival sideshow operator.

At a time when sideshows were still big business, Gibbons charged 25 cents for carnival goers to see what he marketed as "the Ed Gein Ghoul Car. See the car that hauled the dead from their graves."

The car's first gig was the July 1958 Outagamie County Fair in Seymour, Wisconsin (best known for being home of the first hamburger), where it was hidden from view in a canvas tent.

"People want to see this kind of thing," said Gibbons at the time.

Over two days, more than 2,000 people paid the 25-cent admission, almost earning Gibbons' money back for his investment in one weekend.

In Plainfield, the uproar was quick.

"It doesn't sound too good," said Plainville village president Harold Collins. "There's bound to be a reaction. I knew when the car sold for more than it was worth that it would be used for something like this. I don't know what we can do about it. It might open new wounds here."

It was later banned by some fair officials including those in Green Bay, and Gibbons – who by then had more than recouped his initial investment - was forced to tour southern Illinois venues, where the car was not quite as popular and eventually faded into obscurity.

Back to court, 10 years later

After 10 years of confinement, Shubert believed Gein had grown enough mentally and emotionally to stand trial, and he notified Wisconsin Supreme Court judge Robert Gollmar of his opinion. (Gollmar would later go on to write one of the most in-depth books about Ed Gein, simply titled "Ed Gein.")

The trial was set to being on Nov. 7, 1968, and Gein was to be charged only with the first-degree murder of Bernice Worden.

His attorney, William Belter, who had represented Gein 10 years prior, went up against prosecutors Waushara County district attorney Howard Dutcher and Milwaukee attorney Robert E. Sutton.

Both brought psychiatrists. On Gein's side, doctors found him both mentally and legally insane, while a state witness saw him as mentally insane but clinically sane.

Gein continued to maintain that Worden's death was an accident. "I might have pulled the trigger, or it may have gone off by itself," he testified, adding that he couldn't remember the details, in part because the shooting left Worden with a trickle of blood coming out of her mouth. "From little on, whenever I see blood, I'd either faint or black out. That is why I can't remember."

Dr. Milton Miller of the University of Wisconsin described him as "a chronic schizophrenic who sought out the graves of women who resembled his mother "as an attempt on the part of a psychotic and lonely man to bring a form of perverted companionship into his isolated home."

It would ultimately all be nothing but words.

He was found guilty of first-degree murder by Judge Robert H. Gollmar, who said that Gein was savvy enough about guns to have easily "put a bullet" in Bernice Worden's head.

He also "did not check to see if she was dead or alive. He did not do what most people would have done if the shooting was accidental – run out in the street and seek the immediate aid of a doctor," Gollmar said.

Still, so many elements suggested that Gein was truly troubled, and on January 7, 1958 – the same day Russia shot a man 18 miles into space, from where he safely parachuted back to earth - Gein was found not guilty by reason of insanity, and he was ordered to be recommitted to Central State Hospital in Waupun (now known as Dodge Correctional Facility) for an undeterminable term.

He would be somewhere where he would never again be alone.

Gein: The later years

In 1974, he applied for release from the hospital, but was ultimately refused.

According to all reports, Gein was a model prisoner, and eventually in 1978 was moved to Mendota Mental Health Hospital, a low-security facility. Gein had just turned 72.

It was here that officials realized Gein was completely oblivious of his worldwide notoriety.

"Mr. Gein has little insight concerning the possibility that society will remember him and his notoriety, and may continue to respond to him in ways that could be anxiety provoking. He feels that everyone has forgotten him and that he will be able to simply walk away from harassment should it occur. He has some unrealistic plans about going to Australia after being released, although he is not certain about how to arrange his travel plans," said Dr. Thomas J. Malueg during a 1974 interview from Madison's Mendota Mental Health Institute, where he was said to be a model patient. He was 77 years old and at the time of the interview, and had been institutionalized for more than 20 years.

Gein passed away on July 26, 1984, of respiratory failure and was buried next to his mother in the Plainfield Cemetery.

After sightseers continued to chip away souvenirs, Gein's headstone was eventually stolen, only to be discovered in the hands of a Seattle heavy metal band promoter, who was selling rubbings from the stone. Recovered, the headstone became part of the Waushara County Historical Society's permanent collection, and an open spot next to Gein's mother is the only evidence of his grave.

For years, members of the Hill family, the neighbors of Gein who had invited him to dinner on the night he was arrested, continued to leave flowers at the site on Memorial Day.

A never ending trail of visitors

Debby Cave, a longtime employee at True Value Hardware — which was once Worden's Hardware, where Gein killed his last victim - is often reminded of what happened in the 1950s that put quiet little Plainfield on the map.

"My mother's sister was one of those he exhumed," said Cave, in a 2007 issue of Isthmus, the University of Wisconsin-Madison student newspaper.

"It bothers me when I visit my mother's grave," added Cave, who was seven years old when Gein was arrested. "My aunt's grave is nearby, and so is Gein's, although his gravestone is gone."

"People still come in asking questions," she said, "especially the summer tourists and again in the deer season. You see them out on the street, taking pictures of this place. I understand it's part of history, and it's changed now with newer and younger people here. But people for the most part don't want to talk about it, and we're tired of it being dredged up."

A child remembers

While many Plainfield residents chose not to talk about Ed Gein, a boy who knew him later recalled how he felt at the time of Gein's arrest.

"The Stevens Point Journal once carried a quote that said, 'Edward Gein had two faces. One he showed to the neighbors. The other he showed only to the dead.' I think he had many more faces than that. The face I saw as a kid was simply the face of a seemingly normal old man.

"Being a handyman of sorts, Gein kept the farm vehicles in running order, and at times even worked a bit on cars and trucks for other people. When in need of a used part for repairs, if it could not be found in Plainfield, he looked further down the road, sometimes coming to Wisconsin Rapids and to my father's Standard Oil gas station, Whetstone's Highway 73 Garage, just three miles east of Nekoosa in Saratoga.

"We had a fence that bordered the yard, running up to meet at a gate in the northeast corner where Dad's shop was. There was also a drinking fountain at that corner, providing the perfect place for us children to hang out when someone came who might be willing to buy us a candy bar and chat for a bit. Such was the case with Ed Gein. Although I have no firsthand experience in how he interacted with adults, he seemed to like children fine."

Notable inspirations

The story of Ed Gein was so infamous so quickly that he inspired numerous movie and literary characters beyond Robert Bloch's Norman Bates, brought to life on screen by Anthony Perkins.

Others include:

- Leatherface in "The Texas Chainsaw Massacre"
- Buffalo Bill in "The Silence of the Lambs"
- Otis Driftwood in Rob Zombie's "House of 1000 Corpses," who wears a mask made from the face of one of his victims.

David Spanbauer

A monster becomes a remorseless killer

David Spanbauer liked his victims young.

Born, as one judge put it, "a sexual deviant," experts recommended psychiatric care for Spanbauer many times in his life, but it was never enough to stop him from fulfilling his sick urges.

David Spanbauer was born in January of 1941 to Frank and Evelyn Spanbauer, the oldest of three children including sisters Judy and Mary.

The German Catholic family lived near the Fox River, and David struggled to forge a relationship with his father, until the elder Spanbauer died when David was 14.

He then began what would be a lifetime of trouble with the law, including a stint in the Navy that led to three court martials for being absent without leave, which earned him seven months in the brig.

Although Naval doctors believed Spanbauer needed psychiatric care, there was no follow-up, and he returned to

Wisconsin in late 1959 after being dishonorably discharged from the Navy.

The high school dropout attempted to go back to school in Oshkosh, but it lasted only a few weeks.

On January 3, 1960, Spanbauer broke into a home in nearby Appleton, stealing diamond rings, a .22 handgun, a hunting knife, money and a bottle of whiskey.

The next night, he used the stolen gun to rob a home in Neenah.

CHAPTER 1:
Spanbauer was born for bigger crimes

Robbery soon turned out to be much less satisfying, and Spanbauer's crime spree took an ugly turn a week later, when he attempted to rape a 13-year-old girl behind the garage of her home. His plan was foiled when he slapped her and she screamed, but a few days later, his sadistic sexual urges would be finally be satisfied.

16-year-old Carol Grady was playing piano at her aunt and uncle's home in Green Bay, about 45 minutes from Appleton, while babysitting her young cousins.

Peeping Tom Spanbauer, 19, watched her through the window for a while before using his gun to gain entry to the home, and he then dragged Grady to a bedroom, tied her up to the posts of the bed, used a knife to remove her clothing and raped her.

When Grady's uncle returned home, Spanbauer was still inside, and when the uncle walked in to find the deviant inside his property, Spanbauer shot the surprised man in the face, killing him instantly.

It would be almost two months before Spanbauer was arrested, and after facing charges for carrying a concealed firearm, he confessed to the rape and murder, along with the other crimes, saying, "All this started out because I owed two hundred dollars in bills out in California, and I had received the bills presently, the day before."

He went through his entire trial without an attorney, and the prosecutor held out for the longer sentence, saying, "I think the Court must realize that the defendant, to be engaged in crimes such as these, that he must be somewhat ill."

Spanbauer earned a 70-year prison sentence, which he promptly appealed.

His appeal included mental health reports that suggested he was a "very disturbed, extremely dangerous" sociopath who had potential for "an acute psychotic reaction," although his intelligence was not impaired.

It seems a surprise, then, that Spanbauer – whose mother wrote copious letters to the judge, suggesting that Carol Grady was somehow to blame - only served a fraction of that sentence, and was paroled in 1972.

He left prison anything but a reformed man. A tattoo of a devil was now etched on his forearm.

His victim, Carol Grady, wasn't informed of his release, and didn't learn of it until Spanbauer again turned up in the news.

Living the straight and narrow? Hardly

Spanbauer moved to Wisconsin's busy capital city, Madison, home to what was once considered one of the most prominent party schools in the country.

He was living at the YMCA while attending classes at Madison Area Technical College, where he earned good grades even as he found himself hanging out with exactly the wrong crowd.

After loaning his car to an escaped prisoner who used it to flee a robbery, Spanbauer was again arrested, although he was let out on work release, and spent his days working for the Madison Parks Department.

Unfortunately, that meant he was surrounded by pretty co-eds taking advantage of the brief months of summer to soak up some sun on the beaches of Mad Town's four city lakes, each part of Madison's parks department.

The scantily-clad girls caused Spanbauer's sexual urges to resurface, and he did attempt to see a psychiatrist for help.

The professional, however, perhaps unaware of Spanbauer's dark criminal history, shrugged it off, said Spanbauer was likely born "retarded," and washed his hands of the man. In doing so, he unknowingly put several young girls in harm's way. One hopes that at some point he watched the news, saw Spanbauer's face, and realized his horrific mistake.

Next rape results in slap on the wrist

Spanbauer was driving along Hwy. 51 near Madison On Aug. 11, 1972, when he spotted a 17-year-old hitchhiker. The girl was a waitress who was hitching her way home after work. It was late, and she was tired after a long shift.

Instead of making it home, however, she ended up in the car of a madman.

He drove her to the 147-acre Token Creek Park, just north of Madison. On the way, he told the girl he was going to rape her, then run her over with his car and throw her body in a ditch.

The teen started to cry, and then so did Spanbauer. He then tied the girl's hands and raped her.

After Spanbauer tired of the girl, he eventually let her go.

Afterwards, the girl told police that the man who raped her had a tattoo of a devil on his arm.

When police arrested Spanbauer, she identified him as her assailant.

Spanbauer was found guilty by a jury for rape, abduction and sexual perversion, but Judge Richard Bardwell apparently found the crime to be less serious than Spanbauer's first rape, since no one had died in the incident.

While still a sociopath, Spanbauer had shifted from "very dangerous" to "just dangerous, so there has been some improvement," Bardwell said, adding that it was "a very mild rape case," with "no violence."

While the prosecutor had asked for the maximum 50 years on top of whatever sentence Spanbauer would receive for violating his parole from his 1960 rape and murder, Bardwell gave him just 12 years, to run concurrent with his revoked parole.

"The girl was in effect asking for it," said Bardwell in court as he handed down the sentence. "They are tempting fate when they do it."

"I remember being very, very angry after the sentencing," said Dane County Assistant District Attorney John Burr, who said that Spanbauer was "in the top ten of the most vicious and violent people I've ever had the displeasure of coming in contact with."

CHAPTER 2:
Released after 12-year prison stint

Spanbauer left prison with $8,000 he'd earned doing various jobs, and moved in with his sister, Judy.

She was married to Clark Tadych, an Oshkosh police officer, so it seemed as though there would be somebody keeping an eye on Spanbauer.

Instead, the career criminal landed a job at the local Seven-Up bottling plant, and got his own place on Oshkosh's west side.

While Spanbauer kept up with his parole officer – he sent regular letters, describing what he was up to, ending each with the word "Smile!" like a pre-technology version of an emoji – and said he was adjusting well to life outside of lockup, things were boiling under the surface.

A 1991 heart attack on Christmas Eve almost killed him, but doctors revived him, and he went back to the bottling plant.

After work, he would head to a local tavern to drink – bars are prolific throughout Wisconsin, home of Miller, Pabst

Blue Ribbon and Leinenkugel breweries, among others – although he never got too drunk and never caused any trouble, leading establishment owner to say he was a "nice guy."

Laurie Depies: Gone in the night

Winneconne native Laurie Depies was a free-spirited 20-year-old working at Grand Chute's Fox River Mall when she disappeared on August 19, 1992.

She had made plans to meet her boyfriend at his apartment in nearby Menasha after she finished her shift at the mall, and although she made it to the parking lot of his apartment building, she never showed up.

The only clue she left behind was a soda cup left on the roof of her car.

David Spanbauer was later cleared of any connection to the disappearance of Depies. Instead, a week later he encountered Ronelle Eichstedt, a 10-year-old girl out riding her bike, a misfortune that would later lead to Wisconsin truth in sentencing laws that would end early release for good behavior.

The proximity of both time and place would forever linked Depies' disappearance with that of the younger Eichstedt.

A 10-year-old girl on a bike

On August 23, 1992, 10-year-old Ronelle Eichstedt disappeared while riding her bike.

A few weeks later, her blue and pink bicycle was found in some brush near her Ripon home.

"It appears the bike was thrown in from overhead, and not walked in and put back in there," said Fond du Lac Sheriff James Gilmore. "There was no path leading to the bike. Someone threw it from the road."

Ronelle's mother said she was not giving up hope, despite the find.

"In the back of my mind, I still believe that she's alive out there somewhere," Charlotte Eichstedt told the Milwaukee Sentinel. "I can't bear to think anything else."

Six weeks after her disappearance, Ronelle's body was found in a cornfield ditch near Tower Hill State Park, close to the Wisconsin River.

More than 1,500 people attended a memorial for Ronelle Eichstedt at Ripon Senior High School, including teachers, students, police officers and other survivors of tragedy, along with the mother of Laurie Depies.

"I had to come and let them know how much we cared and give them our support and a hug," said Mary Wegner, who was unable to attend the entire service, as her emotions regarding the unsolved disappearance of her daughter were just too raw.

Spanbauer, meanwhile, sold the 1988 four-door Eagle Premiere he had used to transport Ronelle Eichstadt's body.

In its place, he bought a maroon 1991 Pontiac Bonneville.

About seven months after Ronelle Eichstadt's death, her mother, Charlotte, was working third shift at the cookie factory, and her father, Gary, was working construction.

Her sister, Regina Eichstedt, turned 12, and remembered clearly the day her sister disappeared.

The two had been riding their bikes together, until Regina decided to go inside to take a nap. By the time she went back outside, her sister was gone.

"Suddenly there was no Ronnie," Charlotte said. "We have our good days. But we have our bad days, too. Days when it seems like the smallest things irritate us. It's always there, in the back of our minds, no matter what we do. You can't stop thinking about it."

Too, they worried whether whoever took Ronelle would strike again.

"It's frustrating," said Charlotte, "because, to tell you the truth, we're beginning to wonder if they'll ever catch this person, whoever it might be."

It would be another year and a half before they'd have the answers they were seeking.

A predator can't stop hunting

It was a few days after the fourth of July, July 9, 1994, and 21-year-old Trudi Jeschke was home alone at the Appleton house she shared with her sister and brother-in-law.

She had moved there from Michigan about five weeks prior in order to take a job with a bank.

She was on the phone in her darkened bedroom when Spanbauer moved a picnic table beneath the window and cut a screen to gain entry.

He believed the home was empty, but when he entered the room where Jeschke was chatting on the telephone, she screamed, so he shot her in the chest and ran away from the site of the bungled robbery.

"This whole thing raises a lot of anger, of what the parole board used to let him loose," said Jeschke's mother, Linda Jeschke. "I'd give anything if he hadn't been let out."

In 1998, Spanbauer helped lead police to the weapon he used to kill Jeschke. He later ditched the gun at Menominee Park in Oshkosh.

"It doesn't change a lot for our family," said Trish Hummel, Jeschke's sister. "I mean, Trudi's gone either way, with the gun or without the gun, the last four years. But I think it's a final piece to the puzzle. It's nice to know it's done."

CHAPTER 3:
Cora Jones, A bike marks the spot

It was September 5, 1994, and Cora Jones was celebrating Labor Day at her grandmother's house near Waupaca, a town in central Wisconsin that's best known as a recreational area thanks to the nearby Wolf River, a popular spot for canoe trips and tubing.

She had just started seventh grade at Weyauwega-Fremont Middle School.

The older sister to brother Zach, Cora was missing a kidney from a childhood illness, and had plans to become a kidney specialist because of it.

She was, according to her family, "a typical seventh-grade girl."

She liked music, taking on the phone with her friends and playing the French horn in the school band.

She was in Girl Scouts and participated in a variety of church activities, and spent time volunteering with her mother at a local health center.

Her favorite colors were pink and purple.

Fear or premonition?

Ironically, one of Cora's lifelong fears was being kidnapped, and her terror only grew after 10-year-old Ronelle Eichstedt disappeared.

According to her mother, Cora often prayed for Jacob Wetterling, a Minnesota boy who was kidnapped while riding his bike and was featured on a missing poster that hung in Cora's doctor's office.

"We would pray for that little boy. She thought about him a lot," Vicki Jones said.

Two weeks before her disappearance, a man in a car had asked Cora to help him look for his lost dog, prompting Cora, who had watched a video on how to avoid being abducted almost incessantly, until her parents made her stop, said, "No! Are you a creep or something?" and walked away. She later asked her mother, "What would I do if someone tried to grab me?"

While one can never know if it all was a premonition on the part of Cora Jones, her fears came true that Labor Day, when her bicycle was found on nearby Sanders Road, Cora nowhere in sight.

Volunteers come in droves

Hundreds of volunteers were soon combing the area in search of the girl, born Dec. 8, 1981, an early Christmas gift for her parents.

It was "very stressful," said Al Kraeger of the Waupaca County Sheriff's Department. "The family is wondering and you're pulling your hair out asking why, and what for, and what kind of person would want to harm an innocent child."

Five days later, two hunters found her body in a ditch about 75 miles away.

"You wonder how he picked that spot," Kraeger remembered. "It's almost like he wanted somebody to find her."

Jones had been molested, strangled and stabbed.

There was little evidence left behind. Jones was naked and her hands were tied behind her with the scraps of her pink T-shirt.

But there was a carpet fiber, too. And authorities knew the importance of such a clue.

"The case was very personal," Kraeger said. "Anytime there is a case where children are involved, it tears you apart. Is it going to happen again? I'm sure that was a constant thought in everybody's mind. There's fear and sadness for the family. Everybody's guarded and heartbroken. And you hope and pray it doesn't happen to you."

A legacy left in words

Two weeks before she died, Jones asked for a new notebook.

In it, her mother discovered later, were two poems that Jones wrote, her spelling that of a girl still learning.

GOD

by Cora Jones
God is a good word
He is like a spring bird
Don't be afraid to pray
God will forgive you always
He will guide you through life
No matter what road you take
God will always live within you

CRYING

by Cora Jones
It's all write to cry
Just let out a little sigh
Don't be afraid
You've got it made
Cry for love

Cry for hate
I'm just letting you know
Sometimes it's alright to cry.

CHAPTER 4:
Mistakes lead to arrest

"Even before Cora's funeral, I realized the laws need changing," said Cora's grandmother, Elizabeth Schwirtz. Now I live and breathe trying to change the laws."

Meanwhile, on Oct. 20, 1994, Spanbauer raped a 15-year-old girl in her Appleton home, telling her he was not afraid of killing her. Two weeks later, on Nov. 5, 1994, he raped a 31-year-old Appleton woman in her home while her young daughter slept in another room.

Spanbauer was driving a maroon car on July 3, 1994, when he attempted to abduct 24-year-old Miriam Stariha, a small woman in a ponytail who was riding her bike near Hartman Creek State Park.

The car, Stariha said, pushed her off the road and the driver threatened her at gunpoint.

He fled when another car drove by, but Stariha had seen his face, and that would lead to Spanbauer's ultimate arrest.

Officers showed Stariha pictures, and she identified a Madison man as the one who had attempted to abduct her, a mistake that led to news crews and the police swarming the man's home.

"It was unbelievable," said Gary Schmies, a Waupaca County Sheriff's Department detective. "There were cameras everywhere."

After a 10-minute interview, police knew they had the wrong guy.

But they had a photo, and a sketch artist reworked it to make the subject appear older.

It wasn't David Spanbauer, but the photo would prove especially useful later on.

Attempted robbery seals Spanbauer's fate

On Nov. 14, 1994, a man from Combined Locks, a town near the larger city of Appleton, was returning home from an outing when he spotted a guy attempting to break into his house.

He chased the burglar down and tackled him, holding the suspect until police arrived.

The suspect turned out to be David Spanbauer, who was booked into jail on burglary charges.

When police learned Spanbauer was driving a maroon car, he quickly became a suspect in the Hartman Creek incident.

While in custody, the police noticed that the tools found in the suspect's car matched those used in the two home invasion rapes that happened earlier that fall.

They were pretty sure they got their guy, and Langlade County Sheriff's Department Detective Ben Baker, casually brought out the aged composite photo of the Madison man who had been mistaken for Spanbauer. It immediately got the man's attention.

Photo brings ruse crumbling down

"I showed him the picture and knew it hit him hard," said Baker. "He kept looking at it. I put it away and he tried to find it in my papers. Finally he saw it, pointed to it and said it was him."

"The Fourth of July thing. That was me," Spanbauer said.

And although he confessed, he downplayed the event, and said it was nothing more than a misunderstanding.

"I just asked for directions. She had an attitude like I asked for sex or something," Spanbauer said.

He said that she ignored him and rode on, so he grew angry, and hit the woman with his car, knocking her off the road into the brush alongside.

"I was ticked off and was just trying to teach her a lesson. Tell you the truth, it looked more serious than I intended. I was just trying to scare her. It was no abduction thing," Spanbauer added.

But only because another car had driven by, scaring Spanbauer into leaving, had Stariha been given the opportunity to hop back on her bike and ride directly to the police station to report the incident.

In time, a confession comes

Based on the items found in the trunk of Spanbauer's car, along with the carpet fibers that linked him to Cora Jones, the police knew they had taken a dangerous killer off the streets.

But a confession would be like pulling teeth.

The police kept up their interrogations for days, but it wasn't until Spanbauer had secured an attorney, Tom Zoesch, that he confessed to the kidnapping and killing Ronelle Eichstedt and Cora Jones and to the shooting of Trudi Jeschke.

Confessing reveals truth for families

During three days of interviews with Baker and Appleton Police Detective Dan Woodkey, Spanbauer began with the

1992 abduction and murder of 10-year-old Ronelle Eichstedt near her rural Fond du Lac County home.

In his confession, Spanbauer said he saw Ronelle riding her bike near Ripon and forced her into his vehicle, then drove her some miles away and stopped the car. He told her to take off her clothes and tied her hands together before sexually assaulting her.

He then told her to get dressed — leaving off her shoes, socks and underwear — and they drove to a remote area, where he strangled her with a cord, then placed her in the trunk and drove again until he found a wooded spot where he disposed of her body.

Afterwards, he used a knife to cut up the cord as he drove back to Madison.

"I didn't hate David Spanbauer. But I wish I could feel hatred," Baker said.

Spanbauer later confessed to killing Cora Jones, who had feared abduction her entire life.

In his confession, Spanbauer said Jones lived only a few hours after her abduction, and after killing her in the very spot where her body was eventually found by hunters, he "left the body in a ditch and drove away."

During that time Spanbauer would also confess to the murder of 21-year-old Trudi Jeschke during the bungled burglary of her north side Appleton home and two sexual assaults in Appleton.

"His whole reaction to me was, 'those girls were in the wrong place at the wrong time. I just do what I do," recalled Langlade County Sheriff's Department detective Larry Shadick, who regularly visits the memorial left at the site where Cora Jones' body was discovered. "He just was hunting. Like when you go hunting, he found himself a victim."

"I go by the memorial quite often, and it all comes back," he said.

Authorities wondered if Spanbauer had committed other unsolved crimes, and they attempted to question him, including an incident involving a Joliet, Illinois, girl on her bicycle.

"Spanbauer was asked about it," said a detective in the case, "and said 'Where was this? Illinois? Illinois has the death penalty. I don't know anything about it.'"

It brought little comfort to officers, given the severity of his crimes.

"I thought I would feel joy. But this was something you just couldn't get any joy out of," Baker added. "It wasn't a relief. It was just a basic emptiness, a lot like being shell shocked."

Arrest brings back bad memories

Many other people were equally horrified to see Spanbauer's face on television, including a victim that never made it onto Spanbauer's lengthy rap sheet.

"When I was 9 or 10 I was snooping in my parents' bedroom and found a journal and some letters from when my mom was younger," wrote an anonymous poster on cafemom.com. "In it, I read that my mother had been raped. I was so upset and started crying. I confessed to my mom that I snooped and told her what I read. She said, 'yes, that did happen' to her but did not go into any details ... and the subject was dropped.'"

"Just last weekend she was over at my house and she said, 'Remember when you were younger and you snooped and read that letter from my friend that mentioned how I was raped?' I was so surprised she brought it up. (It was something I hadn't thought of in years.) I said, 'Yes, I remember.'

"She said, 'Well, in 1994 I saw the man who raped me on the news. I never forgot his face. I was at work when I saw it, and collapsed to the floor. My co-worker helped me up. I told her, 'that man on the news is the man who raped me when I was 17 years old.' He was on the news because he was charged with raping and murdering a 12-year-old girl.'"

"I was shocked. She was telling me this in such a distant, calm manner. For some reason, I had always thought she was raped by someone she knew, like a date rape kind of thing. I asked her, 'You knew him, right?' She said, 'No, he was a complete stranger. He grabbed me and held a knife to me and dragged me in the woods and raped me. I was able to just fight back and got away. I remember how my hands were bloody from fighting back.'"

"David Spanbauer. He raped my mother in 1972. She was 17 years old and a virgin. She held guilt about never reporting it (though, she didn't know the first thing to do or how to tell police to find him). She said after it happened she was in such serious shock and she just completely shut down. Now, knowing that some girls didn't survive, she is just thankful she survived. I can't imagine how terrifying and horrific that was and am so sad that happened to my mother.'"

CHAPTER 5:
No final trial for David Spanbauer

On Thursday, December 8th, 1994 – the day Cora Jones would have turned 13 - David Spanbauer pleaded no contest to two charges and guilty to the remaining sixteen charges. He was found guilty for first-degree intentional homicide in the Jones and Eichstedt murders and guilty on all other counts.

"Maybe this was our present to her - to get this guy," said Cora's mother, Vicki.

Because he took a plea, there would be no trial.

Still, many attended the Dec. 20 sentencing hearing at the Outagamie County Courthouse, where only two posters were hanging, one offering a reward for information in the murder of Trudi Jeschke, the other a missing persons' poster for Laurie Depies.

The packed courtroom included family members of Cora Jones, Ronelle Eichstedt and Trudi Jeschke, as well as the families of Spanbauer's previous rape victims, who had expected longer sentences for the man who victimized them.

Authorities did not coddle David Spanbauer this time.

Outagamie County District Attorney Vince Biskupic – who would later be found guilty of trial misconduct for bribing prison informants to offer false testimony and hiding evidence - called Spanbauer a "festering soul" and a coward.

"He's evil. And at the same time he's pathetic," said Biskupic.

And with many of the audience watching outside the courtroom via television monitors – the courtroom could hold no more - Spanbauer was sentenced to three life terms in prison without parole, plus 403 years.

"I don't know from what cesspool in hell you slithered forth and I can't send you back," said Outagamie County Circuit Judge James Bayorgeon, who called Spanbauer "pure evil" and questioned why God would allow "a piece of offal like you walk this earth."

Bayorgeon calculated the life expectancies of Jones, Eichstedt and Jeschke when he determined how much time Spanbauer should – and this time would – get.

"What you have done, Mr. Spanbauer, is unthinkable. It is something you must live with for the rest of your days," Bayorgeon said. "The only thing I can hope for is that you never spend one more moment of peace for the rest of your life."

The earliest possible time Spanbauer could be a free man would be December 20, 2191. He would die in prison.

Tell-all falls through

At the time of his death, he was attempting to negotiate a paid interview with the Appleton Post-Crescent, which declined the opportunity because the paper as policy doesn't pay for interviews.

"I think he wanted to cleanse his soul," said his attorney, Thomas Zoesch, who encouraged Spanbauer's confessions so that he could be jailed out of state. Spanbauer apparently feared being killed in prison, since his case was so high profile.

"He had a dark side - kind of a Dr. Jekyll and Mr. Hyde personality," Zoesch said. "The dark side was monstrous and evil. This evil side really controlled him. It wasn't the way he wanted to be, but he had no control over what he did."

Still, Zoesch exchanged letters regularly with Spanbauer, although they stopped for a time when the serial killer developed health problems related to his previous heart attack, and was moved from Minnesota to Wisconsin's

Dodge Correctional Institution, where he could receive better medical care.

"He was always friendly and cordial to me, asking me how I was doing, both personally and professionally. He was an intelligent guy," Zoesch said.

As for his proposed Post-Crescent interview, "I really think he wanted to bare his soul, but there was a monetary motivation as well."

In his last letter to Zoesch, dated July 19, 2002, he wrote, "I want to know if they are going to do it or not.

"Things are getting tight," he added, saying that he was down to the last $100 in his canteen fund.

He died less than two weeks later.

No tears for Spanbauer

"You would be hard-pressed to find someone in the state of Wisconsin who would be shedding a tear over his death," said Outagamie County District Attorney Vince Biskupic. "It's just a shame that taxpayer dollars had to be used to house him for the last several years. This is one of the examples where I and many people in the state would have liked to have had the death penalty option available, based on the repeated and horrific conduct of this despicable man."

As for the families, Spanbauer's death was something they had long anticipated, all the while wondering just how they would react when the news of his death finally came.

"It is kind of a relief. It is a weight off of our shoulders," said Vicki Jones, Cora's mother. "We have been waiting eight years, and we know how bad death is. But after what he did to Cora he didn't deserve to live."

"At least my tax money is no longer going to keep him alive," said Rick Jones, Cora Jones' father. "I always look at my check stub at my taxes and I always knew that I was paying for health care for the guy who killed my daughter. I think we feel now is when he's going to meet the true judge. Judgment will be passed on him one way or another. There will be a party tonight."

There was no funeral for Spanbauer, who was 61 when he died, and no one claimed his body. Instead, a prison chaplain offered a short graveside service.

CHAPTER 6:
The aftermath

In May of 1997, Carol Grady – Spanbauer's 1960 rape victim - led a charge to change laws so felons would be forced to serve the entirety of their sentences, along with a period of supervision that would be a minimum of a quarter of their prison sentences.

"I am angry that someone who perpetuated such a crime is still out there," said Grady. "It irritates me that our laws are such that allows it to happen."

Family members of other Spanbauer victims also supported what would become "two strikes you're out," aimed at those who commit crimes against children. If convicted twice of sexual assault, kidnapping and false imprisonment or incest, it would mean a mandatory life sentence.

"It will never be over," said Debbie Jones, Cora Jones' aunt. "We need to change the laws because we know there's more than just him out there."

A killer confesses

In 2011, Larry DeWayne Hall, 48, a Civil War reenactor from Indiana, confessed to the abduction and murder of 20-year-old Laurie Depies from an Appleton apartment complex.

While Hall, who was serving a life sentence in a North Carolina federal prison at the time of his confession, was not the only person to cop to Depies' disappearance, his story was more credible than most because it included information that was not known to the public.

Hall had been a suspect since he was convicted in the 1993 kidnapping of an Illinois girl.

"From what Larry told us, out of all the other people we've interviewed over the years, Larry seemed the most credible with his information," Town of Menasha Police Lt. Mike Krueger said.

Still, there was not enough evidence to file charges against Hall, and the Depies' case remains unsolved.

Jeffrey Dahmer

Milwaukee cannibal searches for a friend

To hear Jeffrey Dahmer tell it, he was just lonely.

He'd been lonely for quite some time, and for good reason, because around the time when other boys were playing baseball or football, Dahmer was developing an obsession with dead animals. Given that, he and the other kids really didn't have all that much in common.

"He was the loneliest kid I'd ever met," said Derf Backderf, who grew up with Dahmer in the Ohio town of Bath (also the hometown of basketball legend LeBron James), and later wrote a comic book called "My Friend Dahmer," after the serial killer's twisted story of multiple murders and dismemberment with a hint of cannibalism came out.

In desperate need of lasting companionship, Dahmer decided to take matters into his own hands, and embarked on a mission to turn one of the young men he met while trolling Milwaukee and Chicago gay bars into a submissive sex slave who would never leave him.

Funny how things just never seem to work out as planned.

"I should have gone to college and gone into real estate and got myself an aquarium, that's what I should have done," Dahmer later said.

That's the problem with those "should haves." We always think about them when it is much too late.

CHAPTER 1:
Birth of an obsession

Born on May 21, 1960, Jeffrey Dahmer had a fairly normal childhood, until he – like many other serial killers before him – began obsessing over dead animals, a sign that something was amiss for the reclusive young man who by high school had developed a serious drinking problem.

"We found out that he had been collecting at the age of 12 to 14 - you know, when your hormones are ranging, puberty - he was collecting dead animals, road kill, riding around the rural roads and collecting them in bags. His mother didn't know. I didn't know. And apparently, none of his playmates knew," said Dahmer's father, Lionel, in an interview with CNN. "He examined them and he cut into them, cut them open to examine the insides of the animals. And by the way, a lot of people have been telling me that they've done the same thing, but they didn't turn out like Jeff."

Dahmer remembered the first time it started.

"In 9th grade, in biology class we had the usual dissection of fetal pigs," Dahmer said in an interview with Stone Phillips for MSNBC called "Confessions of a Serial Killer," talking about the roots of his strange obsessions. "I took the remains of that home, and kept the skeleton. I suppose it could have turned into a normal hobby like taxidermy, but it didn't."

Hormones and horror

Around the same time, Dahmer's hormones kicked in, and thoughts of sex came as quickly and obsessively as his thoughts of dead carcasses.

"He did what most all of us young males do when the hormones kick in tremendously," said Lionel. "He was doing something sexually with them. And I think the neuronal connections, you know, made contact and sort of hard-wired Jeff, so to speak."

At age 14 or 15, his thoughts turned to violence intermingled with the sex, and he was out of control, with no reason why.

"It veered off into this. It became a compulsion and it switched from animals to humans," he said.

Dahmer became more reclusive, especially at home, where Lionel and Joyce Dahmer's marriage was about to implode.

Dahmer's father remembers his son as being extremely shy during those years, but Dahmer himself says he was shutting down in the wake of his home life, which was becoming a battleground between his parents as they headed for divorce.

"There was so much tension in the home, I didn't really feel like being up and happy all the time," he said. "But I wasn't extremely reclusive. I was a very private person. I liked to keep my thoughts to myself."

Still, Dahmer's father, Lionel, feels profound guilt that he and his then-wife Joyce weren't less volatile, especially in front of Jeffrey and his younger brother, David. (Six years younger than Dahmer, David has since changed his name to distance himself from his deranged older sibling.)

"It makes me sick that we didn't have a more 'Ozzie and Harriet' family," said Lionel. "It makes me sick that it wasn't, and I'll feel that way until my death."

His then-wife Joyce, however, said she didn't think that her fracturing relationship had an impact on the kids, or played a role in Dahmer's coming murder spree.

"Marriage became a very unhappy place, but I didn't think it affected the children, because they were never physically abused," said Joyce, who had been called a "monster maker" for being the mother of one of the world's most notorious serial killers. "It's a terrible feeling and I wish I could come up with an answer. It isn't useful to speculate. I ask the universe why would this be allowed to happen, and I don't have an answer for that. I'd like one."

Drinking doesn't diminish sick fantasies

Dahmer took to drinking, but rather than shutting down his fantasies, the booze made him even more obsessive. The alcohol also diminished any inhibitions his mind might have had, and his fantasies began growing darker and more dangerous with every passing day.

"The subtleties of social life were beyond my grasp. When children liked me, I did not know why. Nor could I formulate a plan for winning their affection. I simply didn't know how things worked with other people…. And try as I might, I couldn't make other people seem less strange and unknowable," Dahmer said.

Still, he played tennis and clarinet in the school band, worked on the school newspaper his senior year, and tried to fit in, even sneaking into the yearbook photo of the National Honor Society as a prank.

But days were difficult for Dahmer at Revere High, and he was almost always drunk. According to classmates, he snuck both beer and hard alcohol into school via the lining of his army fatigue jacket, and despite his extracurricular activities, was generally seen as an outcast.

"It seemed so clear all along that he was someone saying, 'pay attention to me,'" said classmate Martha Schmidt, who remembered Dahmer drinking scotch in class, telling anyone who asked why that it was "his medicine."

But no one did, and Jeffrey Dahmer was essentially left alone with his thoughts.

He graduated from high school in 1978, and on the same day his friend Backderf – creator of the comic strip commemorating his high school classmate - left for college, Dahmer went for a drive.

CHAPTER 2:
Dahmer turns fantasy to reality

It was the summer of 1978 when Steven Hicks decide to hitchhike to a rock concert at Ohio's Chippewa Lake Park.

When he didn't come home the next day, his parents didn't worry, but when six days passed with no word from their son, they contacted police, who retraced the recent high school grad's steps only to find absolutely nothing.

"It was like he had just disappeared," said Carol Hewett-Varner, a detective who would eventually be assigned to the county's only unsolved missing persons case. "It was just the big mystery in this office. What happened to Steven Hicks?"

It turned out to be the worst possible thing. Hicks was picked up by 18-year-old Dahmer, who had been harboring fantasies of stopping for a hitchhiker for as long as he could remember.

"I don't know where it came from," he confessed in the Stone Phillips interview. "I had this recurring fantasy of meeting a hitchhiker on the road and taking him hostage and doing what I wanted to him."

When he saw Steven Hicks, he debated, but his mother had moved, taking his younger brother with her following the divorce, and his father was living in a motel, so "I acted on my fantasies, and that's where everything went wrong."

Dahmer invited Hicks over to drink a few beers, but when Hicks announced it was time to leave, Dahmer decided he didn't want to lose his new friend, and so he hit him in the back of the head with a 10-pound free weight, then strangled him, dismembered his body and buried the remains in the woods behind his father's house.

Many years later, he was worried he hadn't hidden the remains well enough, so he exhumed them, smashed the bones with a sledgehammer and scattered them, where they would mix in with leaves, twigs and the remains of the road-kill animals Dahmer had surreptitiously dissected.

The aftermath of a murder

Later that summer, Dahmer went to college as well, Ohio State University. But because of his drinking, Dahmer flunked out of the university, and was selling plasma to earn enough money to pay for his booze, until his despairing father encouraged him to join the Army.

"I told him, 'There just doesn't seem to be any other way to go right now,'" Lionel told CNN.

For a time, the Army seemed to agree with Dahmer.

"He came back from boot camp looking like just a wonderful physical specimen, smiling, helped me out cutting wood. We were encouraged," said Lionel, who by this time had met his second wife, Sheri.

But it's hard for an alcoholic to quit drinking, especially when trying to suppress memories of murder, along with the fantasies and obsessions that murder had unleashed. So Dahmer drank and dreamed of his next kill.

"Once it happened the first time, it seemed like it had control of my life from there on in," he said.

Dahmer was trained as a medic and assigned to Baumholder, Germany, where he became an angry violent alcoholic.

According to an article in the Independent, he repeatedly raped his roommate, Billy Joe Capshaw, who allegedly returned to his home in Arkansas so damaged that he locked himself in his bedroom for five years.

"I could not say I was raped, I could not do that to my Daddy. He fought in the Pacific," said Capshaw, who told the magazine he spent 26 years in therapy before he was able to speak of his ordeal.

Eventually, Dahmer was booted from the Army, and in 1981 he headed to Florida – the Army had given him a plane ticket anywhere he wanted to go - where he delivered sub sandwiches from a blue van and slept on the beach.

After a few months, he returned to Ohio, and his father did what he could to help Dahmer land a job.

"I would give him my car to go look for a job, and he would end up drinking and leaving the car. He forgot where he left the car many times," Lionel said.

Discouraged, Lionel sent Dahmer to live with his grandmother, Catherine, in West Allis, Wisconsin, a metropolitan suburb of Milwaukee, and he landed employment as a laborer at the Ambrosia Chocolate Factory.

It would mark the start of what would become a murder spree that stunned a nation.

CHAPTER 3:
Second victim opens the floodgates

Steve Tuomi, a native of Michigan who in 1987 was living in Milwaukee and working at a restaurant, was 24 when he ran into Jeffrey Dahmer at a local nightclub.

The two talked for a while before Dahmer told Tuomi he had a room at the Ambassador Hotel and invited Tuomi to spend the night.

When they arrived at the hotel room, Jeff gave his new friend a drink, although Tuomi had no idea it was liberally spiked with sleeping pills. Taking that drink would be the last thing he would ever do.

When Jeff woke up the next morning, he said he found Tuomi's bruised, battered body lying next to him, and had no memory of the events that led to the young man's death.

"When I woke up, my arms were bruised, his chest was bruised and he had blood coming out of his mouth," Dahmer remembered. "I have no memory of beating him to death, but I must have. And that's when the obsession went into full swing."

Dahmer left the hotel to purchase a suitcase, then loaded Tuomi's body into it and enlisted the help of a bellboy to carry the suitcase and its grisly contents to a cab.

He took the case to his grandmother's house, where he secretively dismembered Tuomi's body, smashing bones into smaller bits, then loading the parts into garbage bags that he left out at the curb for the trash trucks.

No part of Tuomi's body has ever been found.

Tuomi's family reported him missing in 1989, two years after his ill-fated encounter with Jeffrey Dahmer.

Trouble at grandma's house

Having killed twice, Dahmer had twice given in to his dark desires, and the hold his fantasies had on him was now that much deeper. And like a drug addict who needs a bigger fix, he found himself going deeper and deeper into the depths of hell with every future kill.

"After the second time, it seemed like the compulsion was too strong and I didn't even try to stop it after that," Dahmer said. "It just escalated, slowly but surely. It took more and more deviant type behaviors to satisfy my urges."

On January 18, 1988, Dahmer spotted 14-year-old James Doxtater, whose Native American heritage included both Oneida and Stockbridge roots.

Albeit young, Doxtater was Dahmer's type – slender and dark-skinned with a shock of dark hair.

Dahmer offered Doxtater $50 to pose nude for photographs after the two met up at a bus stop near a popular Milwaukee gay bar known as Club 219. The boy agreed.

As he had done with Tuomi – and as he would do with every future victim - Dahmer gave the boy, who went by the nickname Jamie and liked to play pool and ride his bike, a drugged drink and then strangled him, stashing his body underneath a blanket in the wine cellar until he had enough time to destroy the remains.

That grisly process again involved acid and a sledgehammer, which Dahmer used to crush Doxtater's bones before placing the remains at the curb for the garbage truck.

Doxtater ended up being the 17th and final victim to be identified by Dahmer, who went through photographs of missing young men during the days following his eventual arrest, since he had successfully disposed of any evidence of his earliest victims.

Killing was a means to an end

According to Dahmer, killing wasn't his main focus when he invited young men back to his place, and he got no pleasure from it.

"I just wanted to have the person under my complete control, to not even consider their wishes. Having total mastery over that person, that was the motive. I wanted to keep them with me as long as possible, even if it meant just keeping a part of them," he said.

To that end, he began saving body parts, especially skulls, although his collection over time grew to include whole heads, hearts and excised muscles stored in his freezer.

"After I left the home, that's when I started wanting to create my own little world, where I was the one who had complete control," he said. "I just took it way too far."

Things begin to escalate

A few months later, on March 24, 1988, 21-year-old Richard Guerrero left his Milwaukee home on the way to visit a friend, carrying little more than $3 in his pocket.

His family never heard from him again.

"Doing something like this, not calling, that wasn't him," said his sister, Janie Hagen, in an interview with the Milwaukee Sentinel after news of Dahmer's arrest led them to question whether or not Richard was one of his 17 victims.

When they found out what happened, it brought both relief and horror.

"It's a relief to know for sure, but then again, in our hearts we knew to expect the worst," Hagen said in a second interview.

On the night he disappeared, Guerrero ran into Dahmer, who invited the young man back to his grandmother's house for beer and to pose for nude photos.

After the two had sex, Dahmer drugged and strangled the victim, ridding himself of the body – at least most of the body - in what was becoming standard fashion, a mix of acid and a sledgehammer to shatter the bones.

Around this time, oblivious to the murders occurring in her home, Dahmer's grandmother found a .357 Magnum beneath his bed and a male mannequin in his closet, both of which freaked her out enough to kick her grandson out of her house.

It was a few months after the murder of Robert Guerrero, but Dahmer, who then found an apartment near the chocolate factory where he worked, was just getting started.

The day after he moved, he was arrested for drugging and molesting a 13-year-old Laotian boy whose brother would later become one of Dahmer's most familiar victims.

Dahmer was convicted of molesting the boy, but sentencing was delayed for a few months, so he temporarily moved back in with his grandmother to await his fate.

Dahmer begins saving trophies

It was the night before Easter Sunday, 1989, and Anthony Sears, a restaurant worker who had just been promoted, was hanging out at the Milwaukee gay bar La Cage when he ran into Jeffrey Dahmer.

The slight candy factory worker invited Sears back to his place, and Sears enlisted his friend, Jeffrey Conners, to give them a ride.

Conners reminded Sears that the next day he was having lunch with his mother, and told the 21-year-old that if he needed a ride in the morning, to give him a call.

Outside Dahmer's grandmother's house would be the last time Conners would see Sears, who was drugged and strangled before dawn.

Dahmer dismembered Sears' body in his grandmother's bathtub.

While Dahmer had previously disposed of his victims, in this case, Dahmer kept Sears' skull and his scalp, because he liked the young man's ponytail. He also kept his genitals, and stored both in a metal box with a lock.

"If I could've kept him longer, all of him, I would have," Dahmer later said of Sears.

A close call

In late March of 1989, while visiting his mother's home, Lionel Dahmer ran across a locked box that he believed contained porn, and he asked Dahmer to open it. Dahmer declined, protesting that he deserved "at least one square foot of privacy," and fled to the backyard.

"I was outside, and I was thinking, 'I've got to stop this from happening. It's all going to come crashing down now,'" Dahmer remembered.

Lionel Dahmer was taking the box to the basement to open it when Dahmer returned, promising to open the box in the morning. Lionel agreed. The next day, Dahmer showed his father the contents of the box, which now contained a plethora of gay porn.

Lionel had no way of knowing that the box had earlier contained the mummified head and genitals of one of Dahmer's victims. Those items, Dahmer then stored in a locker at work, which allowed him to visit his keepsakes during breaks.

"I told Jeff I can't imagine how I would have reacted had I seen what was in the box," Lionel Dahmer said. "I don't know what would have happened. I probably would have lost it."

As for Dahmer, he had yet again gotten away with murder.

"The box wasn't opened, and the lies continued," he said.

Prison term temporarily protects young men

Police had promised the family of Dahmer's Laotian molestation victim that he would be sent away for a long time, so none of the family members attended the sentencing hearing in May of 1989.

"What I have done is very serious. I've never been in this position before. Nothing this awful. This is a nightmare come true for me," Dahmer said at the time. "If anything would shock me out of my past behavior patterns, it's this. The one thing I have in my mind that is stable and that gives me some source of pride is my job. I've come very close to losing it because of my actions, which I take full responsibility for... All I can do is beg you, please spare my job. Please give me a chance to show that I can, that I can tread the straight and narrow and not get involved in any situation like this ever again... This enticing a child was the climax of my idiocy... I do want help. I do want to turn my life around."

Had they been in court, they would have been shocked to learn that Dahmer was sentenced to just one year of jail on work release, which allowed him to keep his job, followed by five years of probation.

His stepmother, Shari, later suggested that his time in prison might have been responsible for his killing spree.

"Something happened to him in prison that he would never talk about," Shari Dahmer said. "Everyone knows what happens to a child molester in prison. I don't know if that's what happened, but, when he came out, he was hardened."

And as much as she might like to believe that, given that he had already racked up several murders, a link between Dahmer's killing spree and short prison term seems unlikely.

Dahmer ended up serving just 10 months of his term, and once it ended, he found a new apartment, this time number 213 at the Oxford Apartments on Milwaukee's east side.

It would become a playground and a museum for Dahmer, and a graveyard for a dozen more young men.

Time away makes Dahmer ravenous

Raymond Lamont Smith and Dahmer had one thing in common. Both were just fresh out of prison – Smith on burglary charges – and were relishing in their newfound freedom.

But on May 20, 1990, 33-year-old Smith - who sometimes went by the name Ricky Beeks – would find that his freedom was not to last.

His family didn't realize he was even missing at first. Smith had told them he was headed to Rockford, Illinois, to visit his daughter, so when they didn't hear from him, they believed he was still across state lines.

It would be more than a year before they would learn that Smith was a victim of Dahmer. The details - he had been strangled and dismembered, his bones stripped with acid before being displayed around Dahmer's second-story apartment as art – would haunt them.

For the rest of the world, Smith would be remembered for little more than the tattoo on his chest, Cash D, and for being the first one of Dahmer's victims to result in cannibalism.

Dahmer later recounted eating Smith's heart, which he said "tasted spongy."

Hunger escalates

Four days later, on May 24, Dahmer was again on the prowl, this time at The Phoenix, another Milwaukee gay bar, one of the most well-established gay clubs in town.

Here, he encountered 27-year-old Eddie Smith, who he lured back to his apartment.

Dahmer later spoke of how sorry he was for killing Smith, in part because his methods of preservation failed miserably – Smith's skull exploded as Dahmer attempted to dry it in the oven – and he was unable to save any mementoes from the crime.

"Edward Warren Smith tried to be Jeffrey Dahmer's friend," said J.W. Smith, brother of victim Eddie Smith.

In 1999, another brother, Ernest, was stabbed to death in his apartment, sending the family back in time to the horrors of losing their first brother to Dahmer.

"It's like living a nightmare all over again," Carolyn Smith told the Milwaukee Journal-Sentinel. "I hadn't really gotten over Eddie's death."

Real-life skeletons in the closet

On September 3, 1990, Dahmer met Ernest Miller outside a gay bookstore on North 27th Street.

He invited the 22-year-old Miller back to his place to watch some porn, and the man agreed.

Unlike his other victims, after removing the flesh from Miller's bones, he kept the man's full-size skeleton in his closet. One of his biceps had been removed and stored in Dahmer's freezer.

Other portions of Miller were consumed.

"His thigh muscle was so tough, I could hardly chew it," Dahmer later told police.

He used meat tenderizer to make Miller's remaining biceps more palatable.

"It was big and I wanted to try it," Dahmer said. "It tasted like beef or filet mignon."

Miller's horrified family later struggled to remain composed in court.

"Jeffrey Dahmer, you have become a hero for a few, but you have become a nightmare for so many more," said Ernest Miller's uncle, Stanley Miller, when the family was allowed to address the killer at his sentencing hearing.

Ill-fated shopping trip

David Thomas was 23 when he encountered Jeffrey Dahmer at a Milwaukee shopping center.

It was Sept. 24, 1990, less than three weeks after Dahmer had killed Ernest Miller and stripped the flesh from his bones.

By now, Dahmer was likely getting cocky. He'd been seen with one of his victims by that young man's friend, and neighbors had to notice the smell of human flesh being eaten by acid from his apartment.

Still, the candy factory worker with the pale skin and hair had not been linked to any of the disappearances of young men in Milwaukee, despite his background as a molester, and he apparently felt free to continue hunting his prey.

Thomas had a girlfriend and two young children, and didn't fit the profile of the other victims.

In fact, after Dahmer drugged the young man, he realized he wasn't really his "type."

Because of that, after he killed him – for fear that Thomas might give him away – he saved no souvenirs, aside from photos he took while dismembering him. The photos were later used by Thomas' sister to identify him.

At his sentencing, Inez Thomas, the victim's mother, told Dahmer, "That was my baby boy you took away from me."

Perhaps Dahmer was unsettled by having to kill Thomas, for having made an impulsive, poor choice, because it wasn't until the next year that his selected a new victim.

Gay advocate's voice silenced

Curtis Straughter was 19 and a member of Gay Youth Milwaukee, a social group for young people who are part of the LGBT community.

He liked to go by the name Demetra, and dreamed of being a model.

Those dreams would be silenced when he encountered Jeffrey Dahmer one day while waiting for a bus near Milwaukee's Marquette University, a private Catholic school that counts late comedian Chris Farley among its graduates.

But the model in him couldn't refuse when Dahmer offered Straughter $50 to pose for photographs.

A few hours later, he would be dead, strangled with one of Dahmer's leather belts.

A brush with necrophilia

Errol Linsey, a choirboy, was 19 years old on April 7, 1991, when he encountered Jeffrey Dahmer outside a gay bookstore, the same one where Dahmer had picked up earlier victim Ernest Miller.

Dahmer offered the young man money to pose naked for photographs, and Linsey agreed.

This time, however, Dahmer had tired of having nothing more than skulls and bones to keep him company.

What he really wanted was a sex slave who would never leave him, and Errol Linsey was his first attempt at making that dream a reality.

"I took the drill while he was asleep," Dahmer said in his confession, which revealed that Dahmer drilled a small hole in the top of Linsey's skull, then used a syringe to inject muriatic acid into his brain.

In the midst of the experiment, Linsey woke up, so Dahmer drugged him again, then strangled him with one of his ties.

He later had oral sex with the corpse, then dismembered it, keeping Linsey's skull as a trophy.

An unlikely victim

Intrigued by the idea of having a sex slave, Dahmer decided he wanted to try again, and on May 24, 1991, he choose deaf mute Anthony Hughes, a 31-year-old man he knew from his visits to local gay bars.

According to Dahmer, he invited Hughes over to pose for photographs, and attempted to turn him into a submissive, again using the drill and a syringe of acid.

Hughes, who was a happy, social guy despite his handicaps, never woke up.

After about three days, Dahmer immersed his dismembered body in acid and saved his skull.

Hughes' mother later disputed Dahmer's claim in court, accusing him of lying about how he had lured the man to his apartment.

"He had four hundred dollars in his pocket that night. He didn't need his fifty dollars," said Mrs. Hughes.

She was likely right.

In a bid to seem less culpable, Dahmer attempted to make most of his victims – the majority of which were young, black men – appear to be prostitutes. He was likely hoping that the courtroom, including the jury, would be less concerned about their lives and deaths if they were sex workers.

Police make a deadly mistake

The family of Konerak Sinthasomphone moved to the United States from Laos in 1980 through the Catholic diocese of Milwaukee, which was assisting with the relocation of Laotian and Cambodian refugees who had escaped communism in their country.

There were four boys, and it appeared that the family would have a better life, until 1988, when one of their sons, then 13, was molested by candy maker Jeffrey Dahmer.

Dahmer was tried and convicted, and police told the Sinthasomphone family that Dahmer would be sentenced to a long prison term, so the family didn't attend his court hearings, and didn't know when Dahmer instead received a year in prison with work release and five years' probation.

The short sentence allowed Dahmer to continue to drug and kill, although he would have been caught much earlier if police had reacted differently on May 29, 1991, when a second son, Konerak Sinthasomphone, was found wandering the streets of Milwaukee, naked, drugged and bleeding.

The two women who found him, Sandra Smith and Nicole Childress, called 911, and officers John Balcerzak and Joseph Gabrish were sent on the call.

They discovered Sinthasomphone - who had managed to escape from Dahmer's apartment from hell when the man had left for more beer - drugged, naked and bleeding from his rectum following a rape.

A returning Dahmer spotted the escapee and told police that the young man was his lover – he produced Polaroids of a half-dressed Konerak to prove it – even as Smith and Childress protested, telling officers they recognized the boy from the neighborhood.

Falling for Dahmer's story, the officers gave Konerak a towel and took him back to Dahmer's apartment. Despite an acrid smell which would turn out to be the decaying corpse of a previous victim, police left the injured boy there.

Later that night, Dahmer killed him, dismembered his body and saved his skull as a memento of the kill.

For the family, their dreams of coming to the United States for a better life shattered, it was horrifying to learn that their lives had twice been impacted by Jeffrey Dahmer.

"We don't have energy to do anything," said Anouke Sinthasomphone, a 27-year-old brother of the dead boy, at the time of Dahmer's arrest. "We can't sleep. We can't eat."

The police officers were later suspended for failing to file a report or check Dahmer's record, but were reinstated when a judge called the suspension too harsh, and "shocking to one's sense of fairness." Both officers were also given $55,000 in back pay following the decision.

And again, the Sinthasomphone family was left to wonder why they had come to America after all.

"They are very confused by the whole thing," said the family's attorney after the officers were back on the job. "They know that their child is dead, and could have been saved."

Apartment of death

After his close call with police Dahmer grew more confident, and killed about one person a week in his attempt to create a zombie-like sex partner who would submit to his every whim.

On June 30, 1991, 20-year-old Matt Turner – a Chicago pizza restaurant worker who loved to lip synch, using the name Donald Montrell – had the unfortunate luck of running into Jeffrey Dahmer at a Gay Pride parade.

Turner, according to those who knew him, was gregarious and friendly, qualities which served him well at his job at the pizza place.

"He was noticeable because he was really outgoing," said Turner's boss, Patti Schuldenfrei, owner of Chicago Style Pizza & Eatery. "He liked to go around to tables and schmooze. I had customers say to me, 'That guy is great. He's so enthusiastic. He's so upbeat.'"

Dahmer likely asked Turner to pose for photographs – according to a friend, Turner loved to have his picture taken – and the two rode back to Milwaukee on Greyhound bus.

Turner never made it back to Chicago.

Instead, he ended up becoming one of Dahmer's failed sex slave experiments.

If at first you don't succeed…

About a week later, Dahmer was ready to try again.

This time, he ran into 23-year-old Jeremiah Weinberger, a customer services rep with an easygoing personality that made him popular both at work and at play.

Weinberger was hanging out at Carol's Speakeasy, a Chicago gay bar, when Dahmer asked him back to his Milwaukee apartment.

Weinberger was intrigued, but uncertain, so he asked a friend what he thought about Dahmer before the two left the bar for the Greyhound bus station.

"He seems alright," said the friend, who according to one report later committed suicide over the guilt of sending his friend to his death.

A former roommate remembered Weinberger fondly.

"He never was in a bad mood," said Tim Gideon, who was working at Carol's the night Weinberger met Dahmer. "I never saw him get mad about anything."

That night, he talked to the two while they sat at the bar, but neither mentioned going to Milwaukee while he was in earshot.

"He wasn't the type of person who would just fly off on a whirlwind vacation," he said. "We never dreamed we'd find him like this."

Unlike many of Dahmer's victims, Weinberger was alive for a few days, acting as Dahmer's boyfriend, and it looked like he might actually survive his ordeal.

Unfortunately for him, however, after a while he tired of Dahmer, and asked to leave.

Dahmer asked him to stay for one more drink.

"He was exceptionally affectionate. He was nice to be with," said Dahmer.

After he fell asleep, drugged, Dahmer injected boiling water into his skull, a new method of making a zombie.

"If they had their own thought processes they might remember that they had to leave, or lived somewhere else," Dahmer said.

Weinberger woke up, disoriented from the drugs and the brain damage, and Dahmer fed him a new drink.

He would end up dismembered, his torso submerged in a large blue vat in the corner of Dahmer's bedroom.

His family became stoic in the face of such a nightmarish discovery.

"We're dealing with it as a family will deal with it," said Weinberger's father, David, owner of Chicago's Caffe Pergolesi, after learning of Dahmer's arrest and that his son's remains were in the Milwaukee man's apartment. "We have a missing person in the family."

Was probation officer to blame?

Weinberger's father later sued the state of Wisconsin and Dahmer's probation officer, Donna Chester, for failing to visit Dahmer's apartment – where she would have seen Dahmer's macabre collection of skulls and bones, and could have prevented numerous deaths including Jeremiah Weinbergers'.

It turns out Dahmer was a model probationer, despite what Chester later said was a deep depression accompanied by regular threats of suicide.

"There were no signs, apparently, no overt signs, no clues, no hints, of a nature that would cause this agent to do anything other than what she did," Joe Scislowizc, a spokesman for the state Department of Corrections later said. "He gave no sign he was involved in any kind of activity of this kind."

At least not until he was arrested.

"Up to this point in time I had no legitimate or lawful grounds under departmental policies and rules to take

Dahmer into custody or to revoke his probation," said Chester. "I never had any grounds to take any disciplinary action against Dahmer or to suspect that home visits would have been of material benefit in his supervision."

Chester had requested that she be allowed to skip home visits with Dahmer, and her request was approved by a supervisor.

Weinberger's lawsuit was ultimately dismissed.

Another tasty victim

Oliver Lacy, 24, had moved to Milwaukee from Illinois with his girlfriend and infant son.

The elite high school athlete – one of the top five runners in the state, he had earned a track scholarship to Texas A&M University, although he had to turn it down because of his grades – was planning on marrying the girl, and would have, most likely, had he not encountered Jeffrey Dahmer at Milwaukee's Grand Avenue Mall.

It was July 12, 1991, and the athletic Lacy caught Dahmer's eye.

He invited Lacy back to his apartment to pose for photographs, and Lacy – likely interested in earning any extra money he could to support his child – agreed.

He was later killed, raped and dismembered, his head stuffed into a box in the refrigerator, his heart saved "for later" in the freezer. His biceps was seasoned with salt, pepper and A1 sauce so it, like the previous biceps Dahmer had consumed, again "tasted like filet mignon."

Lacy's mother knew almost immediately after seeing the news of Dahmer's arrest that her son was one of his unfortunate victims.

"I felt like something hit me real hard," said Catherine Lacy, who confirmed her son's identity by viewing a photograph of his head. "I don't know how this person lured my son. He wasn't the type of person who would let someone come up to him like that."

Dahmer called in sick to work the next day so he would have more time with Lacy's body.

He ended up being suspended, and was fired four days later.

His response was to find another victim to help ease his anxiety over losing the job that paid his rent. He had no way of knowing that it would be his last.

Dahmer's final victim

Dahmer's final victim was 25-year-old Joseph Bradehoft, a married dad of three who was in Milwaukee to visit his brother and try to find work to support his family.

He had just gotten a six-pack of beer when he met Dahmer at a bus stop. It was July 19, 1991.

Dahmer hadn't been sleeping, and was a wreck over the loss of his job. He had purchased a large quantity or muriatic acid in hopes of ridding his apartment of all evidence of his murders, since he was already late with his rent and feared that would soon be evicted.

He likely needed a distraction, and Bradehoft would be it.

Dahmer invited the man back to his place, and Bradehoft accepted.

One drugged drink later, and he ended up becoming a head in Dahmer's freezer, a torso in the acid vat.

"I carried it too far, that's for sure," Dahmer said.

Tracy Edwards ends Dahmer's fantasy

On the night of his arrest, Dahmer lured Tracy Edwards into his home by promising him money and beer for posing naked for photographs.

Instead, Edwards found himself confronted with a knife pointed at his groin, in a room filled with photographs of dead bodies and severed limbs.

"He put his head on my chest, was listening to my heart, and said he was going to eat my heart," Edwards later testified in court.

The two spent time in Dahmer's bedroom watching the movie "Exorcist III," and Dahmer told Edwards how much he hated being alone and worried about other people not liking him.

As he listened, Edwards' mind raced thinking of ways to escape his horrifying predicament.

And as Dahmer talked, Edwards realized he was distracted, so he hit him, leaving Dahmer dazed enough that Edwards was able to escape the apartment of horrors.

Once he flagged down police officers, he was still wearing the handcuffs Dahmer had attempted to subdue him with. The police handcuff key didn't fit, so officers asked Edwards to accompany them to Dahmer's apartment, as he had the key.

Surprises in store

It would be the start of a night that would leave a nation in horror, especially as photos began surfacing over news wires of police carrying a large blue barrel filled with acid-soaked decomposing body parts out of the Milwaukee apartment.

When the officers arrived with Edwards – who then told police that Dahmer had held a knife to him as well – Dahmer told them that the key to the handcuffs was in the drawer of his nightstand.

Officer Rolf Mueller was headed into the bedroom to fetch the key when Dahmer attempted to squeeze past him to get the key himself – and doubtlessly prevent him from discovering the horrible secrets the room contained - and was told by officer Robert Rauth to "back off."

In the same drawer as the key, Mueller found a collection of Polaroid photographs that Dahmer had taken of his victims as he dismembered them.

A dazed Mueller, who realized the photographs were taken in Dahmer's apartment, based on the décor in the background, walked back to the living room, telling his partner, "These are for real."

The photos were gruesome and gory, and the look on both officers' faces likely forced Dahmer to realize his collection was now police evidence.

He attempted to resist arrest, but was quickly overpowered by the two officers, who handcuffed him and called for backup.

Mueller then opened the refrigerator, where he found a freshly severed head.

"For what I did I should be dead," Dahmer said from the floor of his living room.

CHAPTER 3:
Dahmer's house of horrors revealed

Over the course of the night, officials found four severed heads, seven skulls – some painted silver, others bleached – an arm muscle and two human hearts in the refrigerator, a human torso and various organs and bits of flesh inside the freezer, three dismembered torsos in a drum, dissolving in acid, two whole skeletons, a pair of severed hands, two preserved penises and a preserved scalp.

"That any civilized human being in a civilized society could do something this gruesome is inexplicable," said Milwaukee Police Chief Philip Arreola.

"It was more like dismantling someone's museum than an actual crime scene," the chief medical examiner said.

At first, police didn't know how many bodies were hidden in Dahmer's apartment, or how many young men he had actually killed.

"There were virtually no bodies, in most cases, because he had destroyed them," said stepmom Sheri Dahmer. "He had eaten parts, but he had cut them up and destroyed them.

He had put them in trash bags. That's why there was no hard line of bodies to trace."

Instead, they were forced to wade through the morbid bits of evidence.

Milwaukee Mayor John Norquist called it "the most heinous crime committed in the history of Milwaukee."

As for Dahmer, he was in many ways glad his murder spree was finally over.

"I am glad that the secrets are gone," said Dahmer. "I think in some way I wanted it to end, even if it meant my own destruction."

Father's support never wavers

After learning of the circumstances surrounding Dahmer's arrest, Lionel and Shari immediately went to the Milwaukee County Jail where Jeffrey was being held.

"It just seemed like his soul had dropped out of him. I hugged him. And he said to me, 'I really messed up this time,' which is an understatement. And I said, 'Jeff, you really need help. The only way I can see is to have you judged insane so that you'd be put into a psychiatric hospital to really find out what's wrong.' He hesitated at first, but later on, he really wanted to find out what was causing him to do these things," Lionel said.

"I felt depression and shame," Lionel added. "I wanted to help him in some way, and I kept reassuring him. It was sort of a feeling as if I were floating above myself, as if I were anesthetized with something that kept me from feeling anything deeply. It was complete numbness."

Of course, it turned into a circus, the same circus the small town of Plainfield had endured when Eddie Gein was arrested.

"I sat with my mother and ... and our home was invaded by national as well as international photographers set up across the street on neighbors' porches," Lionel recalled. "Ringing doorbells, tromping all over our yard and looking in, trying to see in our windows. It was horrible."

Steven Hicks found

On June 30, 1991, a week after Dahmer was arrested, investigators in Ohio, alerted to Dahmer's first murder, found numerous bone fragments, as well as blood and a bloody handprint in the crawlspace beneath the home where a younger Dahmer had killed his first victim.

Neighbors looked on in abject horror as police struggled to determine which bone bits were human, and which were animal.

"It just shows you how little we knew about them," said James Klippel, who grew up next door and had no idea what had happened in the three-bedroom house formerly owned by the Dahmer family.

A cannibal or a madman?

Much of the media attention was focused on Dahmer's consumption of parts of his victims, their hearts, their biceps.

"It made me feel like they were a part of me," Dahmer later said, "and it gave me a sexual satisfaction for me to do that."

The idea of it inflamed the community, although Dahmer's father said that the dismemberment and the mementoes, those parts of the crimes were much more important to Dahmer himself.

"Actually, the eating part was more like, you know, how the Indians -- the ancient Indians used to eat parts of humans hoping that they would gather strength from that, you know. Jeff told me that that was a very, very small part. It was a part. But very much overblown by the media," said Lionel.

Evaluating madness

Bail was set at $5 million for the man who had peeled the skin off his victims' skulls, at one point attempting to save one of them, saying it resembled a mask at a party store.

Dahmer was immediately seen by a slew of psychologists who attempted to figure out what had gone wrong with the soft-spoken candy factory worker with the blond hair and slightly nasal Midwestern accent.

Most saw him with a degree of sympathy – the lonely boy who desperately wanted someone by his side – and they shared what they believed with Dahmer, giving him some idea of what had caused his world to crack open in madness.

"There is a picture of a lonely, alienated small boy who has a difficulty relating to anyone," said psychologist Samuel H. Friedman, who later disputed Dahmer's insanity plea at trial.

"I knew I was sick or evil or both. Now I believe I was sick. The doctors have told me about my sickness and now I have some peace. I know now how much harm I have caused. I tried to do the best I could after the arrest to make amends," he said.

While he was in jail awaiting his trial, he read books his father sent him, and he began looking to God for answers.

"I now know I will be in prison the rest of my life. I know that I will have to turn to God to help me get through each day. I should have stayed with God. I tried and failed and created a holocaust," he said. "Thank God there will be no more harm that I can do. I believe that only the Lord Jesus Christ can save me from my sins."

Lionel Dahmer worried that his son would want to commit suicide given the bleakness of the situation, and was unable to come to terms with his son as the evil, deranged man the media portrayed.

"I can remember him as a youth, when he was innocent," said Lionel. "The naïve parent in me still sees an innocent, shy child."

Eventually, the victim list reached 17, over the span of more than a decade, and his parents began debating what they might have missed during Dahmer's childhood that might have predicted his future crimes.

Lionel Dahmer, who was bullied as a child, had dreams of murder, and debated if he had perhaps passed a genetic propensity for killing on to his son.

Stone Phillips, who later called the interview one of the more unsettling of his career, especially after Dahmer took time out as he left to point out a box, saying it looked exactly like the one whose contents he had carefully hidden from his father - asked whether Dahmer thought family problems led to his lifestyle. Dahmer was quick to reject the idea.

"I think it's wrong for people who commit crimes to shift the blame to their parents, to their upbringing," Dahmer said. "I think that's a copout. I take full responsibility. I just get angry with other people who try to blame my parents for what happened. I alone am the one who's responsible for what happened."

In fact, he credits his parents and their undying love for carrying Dahmer through the dark days of jail, of his trial and of what he believed would be a lifetime in prison.

"Without the support of my folks, I don't think that I could have come through this," said Dahmer, who said that the family conversations are deeper now.

"There's a lot more communication between us," he said.

Still, his fantasies of death and dismemberment lingered, a darkness in his brain that tortured him daily.

"It never completely goes away," Dahmer said. "I wish it would go away. It will probably be with me for the rest of my life."

CHAPTER 5: The trial of Jeffrey Dahmer

Lionel Dahmer wonders how he and his wife, Shari, managed to make it through the trial, much of which focused on whether Dahmer was sane or insane, especially as they learned he often had to shower with corpses he kept hidden in the tub, because they were piling up at his place so fast.

"We sat just motionless and sick to our stomach," Lionel said. "To this day, I can't really see how I -- we both just sat there."

Dahmer sat with his attorney, his back to his family.

Meanwhile, psychologists debated back and forth.

"Most people that have even severe mental illnesses are not dysfunctional in every aspect of their lives. Many work, get up in the morning, they dress, they shower, they watch TV, they read the newspaper. They may become psychotic only during periods of severe stress," said Dr. Carl Wahlstrom, who testified at the Jeffrey Dahmer trial and later spoke to the Chicago Tribune. "I think Jeffrey Dahmer had both borderline personality and schizotypal personality disorder. Part of the characteristics of those disorders is that under severe stress someone can become psychotic, and that could be an internal or an external stress. His personality structure is extremely primitive. He has bizarre and delusional ideas."

Others said Dahmer's inability to interact well with others as a child suggested he might have had Asperger's syndrome, a form of autism.

In fact, Wahlstrom later said that if mental health professionals had noticed the extent of Dahmer's problems, they could have helped him before he turned into a murderer.

"He was very ill from childhood on," Wahlstrom later said. "There was a question in one of the cases I read. One probation officer had referred him to some treatment, and he had been treated by a psychologist. He wasn't really cooperating, he was just going through the motions. Had that psychologist said 'Just showing up is not enough. I'm going to say that by not participating in treatment I think that you're violating the conditions of probation. I'm going to recommend that your probation be violated unless you start talking to me.' That's Monday-morning quarterbacking a bit, but I think that had his problem been recognized in early childhood, it's possible that someone with such a profound self-esteem problem could have been helped, so it didn't get to where it did. He really didn't feel that he could talk to anybody about what was going on in his mind after a point, and he began to lead an increasingly private existence filled with fantasies and delusions."

Others suggested it was borderline personality disorder, because despite being the aggressor in each of his crimes, Dahmer saw himself as a victim as well.

"What I've done has cut both ways. It's hurt the victim, and it's hurt me," "Dahmer said. "I don't know what I was thinking when I did it. I know I was under the influence. It is hard for me to believe a human being could have done what I've done."

Others said he killed in order to silence his own homosexuality, which was something he hated and refused to admit about himself.

But Dahmer, Wahlstrom said, was more likely unable to figure out a way to forge a relationship with another man, given his difficulty in making friendships as a child.

"He liked other men, and he was completely ineffectual and could not even conceptualize what a relationship would be with someone. And so he attempted, in whatever way he could, to form something," Wahlstrom said.

Insanity plea hard card to play

But insanity was a different story, and many believed he was not insane at the time of his crimes.

"Jeffrey Dahmer knew exactly what he was doing. He took precautions. He knew the consequences of his actions. But he did not want to stop," said forensic psychologist Dr. George Palermo. "Nobody can deny that Jeffrey Dahmer is a sick person. (But) he is not psychotic. He was legally sane at the time of the offenses."

Too, he was able to deliberately deter police when they were at his apartment with Konerak Sinthasomphone, even though if one of them had opened his bedroom door, they would have discovered his macabre collection.

"He fooled everyone. He had bodies in his next room when the police were standing in his outer room," Lionel said in the Stone Phillips interview. "There were so many people that he fooled. He just looked very innocuous, he looked like an average person who couldn't possibly do the things that de did."

A madman in disguise

Inexplicably, family members of the victims agreed.

"He wasn't what I expected," said Therese Smith, whose brother, Eddie Smith, was one of Dahmer's victims.

"He didn't seem evil or anything," said Shirley Hughes, whose son, Anthony, had known Dahmer for years before becoming one of his victims. "Just to look at him, you wouldn't think he could do the types of things they've said he's done."

"I know the families of the victims will never be able to forgive me for what I have done," Dahmer said in court. "I promise I will pray each day to ask for their forgiveness when the hurt goes away, if ever. I have seen their tears, and if I could give my life right now to bring their loved ones back, I would do it. I am so very sorry."

It took a jury just five hours to find Jeffrey Dahmer sane and reach a verdict in the case.

He was sentenced to life in prison.

Dahmer lamented his future.

"I couldn't find any meaning for my life when I was out there, I'm sure as hell not going to find it in here," Dahmer said. "This is the grand finale of a life poorly spent and the end result is just overwhelmingly depressing... it's just a sick, pathetic, wretched, miserable life story, that's all it is. How it can help anyone, I've no idea."

At the hearing, family members were given a chance to speak, and one made national news for screaming "I hate you, Jeffrey" at the top of her lungs as she was held back by bailiffs.

Still, he was unable to speak directly to the families of his victims, and said nothing when they raged at him during his sentencing hearing.

"Any words that I could say to the victims' families would just feel trite and empty," he said. "I can't find the right words."

He did, however, mention his family as he took responsibility for what he had done.

"I know my time in prison will be terrible, but I deserve whatever I get because of what I've done. I've hurt my mother and father and stepmother. I love them all so very much. I hope that they will find the same peace I am looking for," he said.

He later pled guilty to aggravated murder in Ohio, in the death of his first victim, Steven Hicks. He was again sentenced to life in prison without parole.

CHAPTER 6:
The aftermath

Over the years that Jeffrey Dahmer was imprisoned, Lionel Dahmer visited his son about once a month. They never talked about Dahmer's crimes.

"There's no point to going into in-depth talks about it," said Dahmer. "We talk about family, how things used to be. It gives me a sense of comfort to talk about the few good times we had in the past."

Dahmer was beaten to death at Wisconsin's Columbia Correctional Institute by fellow inmate Christopher Scarver in 1994, in part because Dahmer spent his time in prison taunting other inmates with dioramas of his crimes fashioned from his prison dinners.

Scarver – who had been housed in prison with Dahmer since 1992 for killing his boss in 1990 – said Dahmer would create severed limbs from his food, then drizzle them with packets of ketchup, leaving them in places where they would be easily noticed.

"He crossed the line with some people — prisoners, prison staff," Scarver told the New York Post in 2015.

"Some people who are in prison are repentant — but he was not one of them," Scarver said.

An attorney later told Lionel Dahmer that he believed Scarver and Dahmer were deliberately left alone for the minutes required for Scarver to make his move.

"This attorney said he was confident that it was something that was allowed to happen, as he put it," Lionel said. "And for the second time I sat at my desk, totally numb, paralyzed, to get - to get the news."

A sandwich still causes nightmares

Eighteen years after Jeffrey Dahmer died, his former neighbor Pamela Bass recalls eating a sandwich Dahmer gave her one day, its contents unknown.

"I have probably eaten someone's body part," Bass told documentary filmmaker Chris James Thompson, who also spoke to Police Detective Patrick Kennedy, who blames the Dahmer case for his divorce, and Milwaukee Medical Examiner Jeffrey Jentzen, who has images of items found in Dahmer's apartment seared into his memory bank.

Thompson was making the documentary "The Jeffrey Dahmer Files," which was released in 2013.

Did Dahmer kill Adam Walsh?

In October of 2015, a book by former Miami Herald press operator Willis Morgan was released, suggesting that Dahmer had kidnapped six-year-old Adam Walsh from a Florida mall.

In "Frustrated Witness," Morgan recounted recognizing Dahmer immediately as the man he had seen in the mall the day Walsh disappeared when his mugshot appeared in the paper following his Milwaukee arrest.

Walsh's decapitated head was later found off a main highway. His murder became one of the most well-known unsolved crimes in U.S. history after his father, John Walsh, introduced the world to "America's Most Wanted," a show designed to track down killers to prevent others from living with the horror of the unknown.

Morgan, however, thinks that he holds the key to the murder case, which ultimately was pinned on another man.

At the time of Walsh's disappearance in 1981, Dahmer was living near Miami Beach, and as a sub shop delivery person, had access to the blue van that witnesses reported seeing leaving the mall.

He also matches the description another woman gave to police after her son was nearly kidnapped a week before Adam Walsh.

John Walsh himself agrees that there is plenty of evidence suggesting that Dahmer could have been responsible for his son's death.

"Many people have forgotten that Jeffrey Dahmer started out as a pedophile, kidnapper, and torturer of young boys," said Walsh in a letter that was included in a Milwaukee news story speculating about the link. "He certainly fits the profile of someone who might be capable of murdering a beautiful 6-year-old boy."

Florida police did interview Dahmer, and determined there was no evidence against him, despite numerous witnesses describing him almost exactly.

"In 1992 I gave up trying to convince people," he told Fusion. "I had called every newspaper, every TV station, anyone who would listen, and told them the story. And the one reporter who actually listened to me called me back and said 'The police department has eliminated Jeffrey Dahmer as a suspect.'"

Walter Ellis

DNA mistakes almost let him get away

For more than 20 years, between stints in prison, Walter Ellis was roaming Milwaukee's North Side, terrorizing women and earning the nickname the Milwaukee North Side Strangler for the women he killed between 1986 and 2007.

He was able to get away with his crimes for so long because he, like many other serial killers before him, sought out victims who were less likely to be missed.

"The victims were prostitutes. They had drugs in their system. They had multiple sources of DNA," said Milwaukee homicide detective Steven Spingola.

Because he chose sex workers as his victims, Ellis was able to evade capture for decades, much like other serial killers who sought out prostitutes to satisfy their urges.

"I picked prostitutes as victims because they were easy to pick up without being noticed," said Gary Ridgeway, who killed dozens of prostitutes working the Seattle area over his two-decade murder spree. "I knew they would not be reported missing. I picked prostitutes because I thought I could kill as many of them as I wanted without getting caught."

Others chose sex workers because they felt it was their duty to rid the world of evil, although for those unlucky enough to hook up with a madman, the true evil was something else entirely.

Even more unsettling, all of them walked into their deaths willingly in the hopes of making a few bucks, maybe to support a drug habit, maybe to support their children.

And they had no idea that they were hooking up with a madman when they met with Ellis, he added.

"They were choked and they apparently went with him willingly up until the point the homicides occurred," said Spingola.

It was an unfortunate night on the job for nine African-American sex workers, but serious mistakes by Wisconsin's criminal justice system ensured that it would be decades before their killer was caught.

CHAPTER 1:
DNA mistakes slow arrest

Ellis had been arrested numerous times throughout his 21-year murder spree, and should have had DNA samples in a state database. As it happened, when he was supposed to give a sample, he apparently enticed another inmate to give one in his place, keeping his own DNA profile from being available.

Even more disturbing, the DNA discrepancy was discovered, but was not rectified, leaving Ellis' DNA out of the system despite his lengthy arrest record and history of anger.

"Yes, he does have a criminal history," said Milwaukee Police Chief Edward Flynn after Ellis' arrest. "His criminal history, however, does not lend one to immediately say, you know, 'prime suspect.'"

Ellis' charges include violent and property crimes, although his last conviction came in 1998, two years before DNA samples were legally required.

He was arrested for the 13th and final time when police executed a search warrant at his apartment and took samples of DNA from his toothbrush that matched DNA found on all eight known murder victims.

He was arrested a day later at the Park Motel in the Milwaukee suburb of Franklin after a struggle with police and charged with two counts of first-degree intentional homicide.

Police downplay mistakes

Police downplayed the DNA errors that allowed so much time to go by between Ellis' first murder and his last, and instead pointed out the work they had done to finally catch the man who had terrorized Milwaukee for so many years.

"Good police work and good police science have led us to Walter Ellis," Flynn said.

"I'm glad they got this man, because I just feel sorry for what my sister went through," said Tara Noble, whose sister, Joyce Mims, was one of Ellis' last victims. "We just think about how she was killed. My sister was found beaten and strangled. Those are words you don't ever want to tell somebody."

Not who he seemed

An anonymous neighbor who lived downstairs from Ellis' duplex apartment on Bobolink Avenue, a place he shared with his girlfriend Tressie Johnson, said what people always seem to say when they live near or know someone who turns out to be a serial killer.

"He didn't seem like that type of person," said the woman, who said she saw the two on a daily basis. "It's so scary now. I could have been a victim. I'm shaking right now."

CHAPTER 2:
Victim list spans 20 years

Debra Lynn Harris, 31, had moved to Milwaukee in hopes of a better life.

Her friend, Patricia Donald, called Harris a generous, loving person, who deserved nothing but a bright future.

Instead, she would wind up dead, strangled with a black and white handkerchief and tossed into the murky waters of the Menominee River on Oct. 10, 1986.

It was the start of what would be a ravenous killing spree for Walter Ellis, who would spend decades as a free man while family members of his victims waited and worried.

"He did not suffer enough for that family," said Terry Williams, whose sister, Joyce Mims, who would later become one of Ellis' victims.

One day later, a second victim dies

In reality, Walter Ellis had developed a taste for murder, and after the first one, the second one – a day later on Oct. 11, 1986, was that much easier.

Tanya Miller was 19 when she died in a Milwaukee backyard.

Bill Vogl, a detective with the Milwaukee Police Department's homicide unit, immediately suspected that both women had been killed by the same person.

"I used the word serial, and I got reamed out," Vogl remembered. "That was the end of the meeting. They didn't want the word used. They didn't want that to get out to the media."

Just like so much trash

On November 28, 1992, the body of Irene Smith was found dumped in a trash bin in an alleyway, bearing stab wounds to her neck and evidence of strangulation.

Because she was stabbed, she was the first victim whose death deviated from a pattern established by Ellis in 1986 when he killed his first two victims.

But she was found in the 3000 block of N. 6th Street, where Ellis lived with his mother at the time.

She would be one of many victims found in that area, and if Ellis' DNA had been in the system, he might have been caught much sooner.

As it happened, many more women in and around the neighborhood would have to die before Ellis would be caught.

DNA match not enough for arrest

Although Ellis' DNA was found on the body of 32-year-old Carron D. Kilpatrick, who was murdered in October of 1994, Ellis was not definitively linked to her death.

Instead, despite Kilpatrick's body turning up in a trash bin in the same alley where Irene Smith's body was found, her live-in boyfriend, Curtis McCoy, with whom the mother of five had a daughter, was targeted as a suspect.

It didn't help that a man who lived with McCoy said he heard the two arguing before seeing McCoy drag Kilpatrick's body into his van, or that Kilpatrick's five-year-old daughter said she also saw McCoy drag her mother's body out the front door.

"There was an overwhelming mountain of evidence against him," said his defense attorney, Michael L. Chernin.

That evidence included what amounted to a confession, coerced out of a distraught McCoy by two detectives who'd gained his trust.

"Curtis was so distraught at the time they more or less convinced him through just talk therapy that maybe he was temporarily insane at the time," Chernin said.

Meanwhile, Chernin's investigators were poring over case files similar to Kilpatrick's, and believed that it might have been the work of a serial killer, information that was not allowed to be used in McCoy's criminal defense.

Despite the evidence, McCoy was acquitted of Kilpatrick's murder, and he moved away to escape the notoriety. Kilpatrick's death has now been unofficially linked to Walter Ellis, cementing the serial killer theories tossed about by Chernin and his investigative team.

Abandoned

On April 24, 1995, workers doing repairs at an abandoned house found the body of Florence McCormick dead in the basement, her wrists tied with a rope that was secured to a washtub sink.

The rope also was wrapped around her neck.

It was a sad, lonely place for the 28-year-old mother of two daughters to die.

But she would not be the only woman to be left in an abandoned house.

On June 27, 1995, the body of Sheila Farrior was also found in an abandoned house, her bra wrapped around her neck.

The mother of five had been strangled, leaving behind nothing but questions for her family.

"Obviously, I can't say it was given a high priority," said Farrior's father, Sandy Farrior, in a 1997 interview with the Milwaukee Journal-Sentinel. "They can't do anything for my daughter, but perhaps they can prevent the deaths of others."

Unfortunately, they couldn't. Police had failed to acquire accurate DNA samples during the 12 times Ellis was in prison, including for assaulting his girlfriend with a hammer, and when he served as a government informant in order to spare himself jail time. There was nothing in the system to match future victims.

"Had it been a Caucasian lady, that killer would have been found," said Shannon Farrior, who was 17 when her mother died. "I don't understand how would a killer not make no mistakes that you can't get a lead on him in 14 years. I know he's not that clever."

Zola Farrior, Sheila's sister, called Ellis "nothing but the devil."

"He didn't only kill my sister, he killed my mother - she died of heartbreak after that," Farrior said.

Hiding behind a new M.O.

Ellis only strayed from his modus operandi once, and that was when he killed 16-year-old Jessica Payne.

Her body was discovered beneath a discarded mattress behind a vacant house on Aug. 30, 1995. She had been raped and strangled, and her throat was slit.

The white teen was a runaway with a drug problem, and her murder was initially pinned on another man, Chaunte Dean Ott, who was convicted of first-degree murder after a friend's confession linked him to the crime.

Ott spent 13 years in prison before DNA evidence determined a link between Payne's murderer and two other victims of Milwaukee's North Side Strangler.

Ellis, however, was never charged in Jessica Payne's murder.

Too close for comfort?

On June 20, 1997, the body of Joyce Mims was found in a closet in an abandoned Milwaukee-area house, bruising on her chest and face.

An autopsy later determined that she died from manual strangulation, an intimate and sadistic crime that allows the killer to be fully engaged during the passage from life to death.

She was dating Ellis' uncle at the time of her death, and everyone knew her killer, including her son, Purvis Mims, who had met him about six times.

"He just seemed like a regular guy," he said. "It goes to show you never know what's going on behind closed doors."

Being that close to a killer, however, turned out to be a fatal mistake for Mims.

"I know she wouldn't have gone in an abandoned house with a stranger, regardless of the circumstances," said Purvis Mims. "She probably had a rapport of some fashion with him."

Purvis Mims also said he was optimistic that police would eventually find his mother's killer.

"I was pretty confident because a person who does those types of things, they don't stop," he said. "You don't just never do it again or never have any police interaction."

"We just hated that it had taken so long for them to find her killer," said Mims' brother, Terry Williams. "But you know, justice one day is better than no justice at all."

Another prostitute chooses wrong mark

Milwaukee prostitute Maryetta Griffin was found strangled to death on Feb. 17, 1998, lying in a pile of garbage in a Milwaukee garage.

DNA samples taken from Griffin's body matched Walter Ellis, although he was never charged with her murder.

Another man, William Avery – who operated a crack house near the home where Griffin's body was found and was Griffin's dealer - was a suspect in Griffin's murder, but because there was no solid evidence, he was instead arrested on drug charges and sentenced to 10 years in prison.

It wasn't until other inmates told police Avery had confessed to the crime that charges against him were brought, although police should have taken the inmates' information with a grain of salt.

"The problem with jailhouse informants is credibility," said Steven Spignola, who wrote extensively about Walter Ellis. "Most are convicted felons serving time for serious crimes. In some instances, offenders game the system to seek reductions in their sentences or assignments to a correctional facility with better living conditions. Ultimately, it is up to the jury to ascertain whether these inmates are telling the truth. These surly individuals are generally not

Eagle Scouts out to do the right thing by stepping forward as witnesses."

Avery later asked for a specific DNA sample taken from Griffin's body to be tested, and it came back a match for Ellis.

"We're going to have to re-examine any cases that fit a general profile and make sure that we re-examine the integrity of all those cases to make sure that we're satisfied that justice has been done," said Milwaukee County District Attorney John Chisholm.

Making sure to leave evidence behind

Quithreaun Stokes did not go quietly, and because of that, police were finally able to close in on Walter Ellis.

When officers found her body on April 27, 2007, a can of pepper spray was discovered nearby, suggesting that she attempted to fight back when her assailant ripped her clothing partially off to rape her before strangling her with his bare hands.

Police gathered evidence including fingernail clippings from the victim to capture any DNA from defensive actions as well as the pepper spray can, which was colored with a smear of blood.

That blood helped seal the fate of Walter Ellis, finally, after so many years.

It also helped solidify homicide detective Vogl's long-held belief that Milwaukee was dealing with a serial killer.

"These types of people have something obviously wrong with them in their minds," Vogl said. "I don't know what gratification they get from doing it, but they don't stop. That's a true serial killer. They don't stop."

CHAPTER 3:
Trial a farce for victims' families

Walter Ellis initially pleaded not guilty to the murders, and told a judge that when his attorney, Russell Jones, came to see him, they didn't talk much about his case. After Jones was then dismissed, Ellis prepared to defend himself in court.

Ellis announced twice that he would enter a plea deal, eliminating the need for a trial, but both times he backed out at the last minute.

Family members of the victims believe that it was a deliberate move by Ellis to torment them one more time, but the sister of victim Irene Smith told the Milwaukee Journal Sentinel that she was not going to allow Ellis to get to her.

"He's not going to psych me out anymore," said Virgie Smith-Norwood. "He's sick."

"We're going to all be all right. You don't win. You don't get to destroy lives anymore," said Debra Harris' friend, Patricia Donald.

Eventually, on Feb. 19, 2011, Ellis entered a plea of no contest to seven intentional homicides, a plea that immediately resulted in a conviction.

A week later, on Feb. 24, 2011, he was sentenced to seven consecutive life sentences without the possibility of parole.

He never spoke publicly about his crimes.

"Everyone wants to know why," said Milwaukee County Circuit Judge Dennis Cimpl at the time of his sentencing. "Unfortunately, Mr. Ellis has the right not to tell us."

After spending a few months first at the Dodge Correctional Institute in Waupun, then at the Wisconsin Secure Program Facility in Boscobel, he was transferred to a maximum custody unit at the South Dakota State Penitentiary.

He died in a South Dakota hospital on Dec. 2, 2013, of natural causes, taking with him a wealth of secrets.

"Why he wanted to kill these women, it'll go with him to his grave here. He would have been an interesting person if he would have decided to sit down like Bundy at the last minute if he knew he was dying and clear his soul, but nothing," detective Spingola said after his death. "I just wonder about the other cases that he was mentioned in. There's at least five, maybe seven more that he's a good suspect in that we'll probably never know."

Conclusion

So, is it the Wisconsin winters that drive men to madness, or is it entirely a coincidence that two of the most bizarre, horrifying and heinous serial killers are from the same part of the country?

It seems so unlikely.

But still, Steven Avery – a man who was falsely imprisoned for 18 years for a rape he didn't commit, later winning $36 million from Manitowoc County for his time in prison – later lured Teresa Halbach to his home to take pictures of a car he was selling, only to rape and murder her, burning her body to hide the evidence and enlisting his nephew to assist.

He claimed that evidence was planted, but Halbach's teeth and fragments of her bones were found in his fire pit, making that an impossibility.

Avery could have spent the rest of his life drinking tropical drinks with umbrellas on a beach in the Bahamas, but instead, he's back behind bars.

Clearly, something isn't right in America's Dairyland.

What it is, however, only those who live there can know for sure.

More Books by Jack Rosewood

When Chris Bryson was discovered nude and severely beaten stumbling down Charlotte Street in Kansas City in 1988, Police had no idea they were about to discover the den of one of the most sadistic American serial killers in recent history. This is the true historical story of Robert Berdella, nicknamed by the media the Kansas City Butcher, who from between 1984 and 1988 brutally raped, tortured and ultimately dismembered 6 young male prostitutes in his unassuming home on a quiet street in Kansas City.

Based on the actual 720 page detailed confession provided by Berdella to investigators, it represents one of the most gruesome true crime stories of all time and is unique in the fact that it details each grizzly murder as told by the killer himself. From how he captured each man, to the terrifying methods he used in his torture chamber, to ultimately how he disposed of their corpses - rarely has there ever been a case where a convicted serial killer confessed to police in his own words his crimes in such disturbing detail.

Horrific, shocking and rarely equaled in the realms of sadistic torture – Berdella was a sexually driven lust killer and one of the most sadistic sex criminals ever captured. Not for the faint of heart, this is the tale of Robert "Bob" Berdella, the worst serial killer in Kansas City History and for those that are fans of historical serial killers, is a true must read.

This is the story of how on April 28th, 1996, a lone gunman with no warning, walked into a crowded café in the historical museum site of Port Arthur and opened fire on unsuspecting tourists with a semi-automatic assault rifle.

By the time Martin Bryant's was captured nearly 24 hours later, his killing spree would claim the lives of 35 people and wound another 23 before he would finally surrender to Australian police. The massacre would become the most violent mass shooting in Australian history, committed by a 28 year psychopath with a long history of mental disorders including schizophrenia and depression.

In this Australian true crimes investigative report, you'll relive the shocking true story of the Port Arthur Massacre including an in-depth analysis of Bryant's bizarre behavior leading up to his murderous rampage that killed men, women and children in cold blood. Written in vivid graphic detail, this is the story of the events that unfolded as told from the accounts of those that witnessed and survived one of the worst mass murders in Australian history.

More Books by Dwayne Walker

In the decades between the American Revolution and the American Civil War, the United States government was engaged in an ongoing war against several Native American tribes. Collectively, historians refer to the series of wars between the U.S. government and the American Indians simply as "The Indian Wars," or "The American Indian Wars." The Americans argued that they needed the land west of the Appalachian Mountains for development and settlement, while the various American Indian tribes argued that the land was their birthright; both sides were willing to shed blood to accomplish their goals!

Perhaps the greatest series of battles between the Americans and Indians was the Northwest Indian War (1785-1795), which took place in what was then known as the Northwest Territory and what today comprises the states of Ohio and Indiana. On the one side was a modern army, ready to conquer the land, while on the other was a coalition of Indian tribes who were much better organized and equipped than their adversary believed. The result of the war proved to be a turning point not only in the history of the United States, but also in Native American History.

The highpoint of the war for the Indians and the low point for the Americans was a battle often referred to as the "Defeat of St. Clair" for the American general who lost hundreds of men in a well-organized massacre to Indian forces led by chief Little Turtle. The following book brings St. Clair's defeat to life in a way that has never been done before by using historical documents combined with Native American tales to create a narrative that is as exciting as it is edifying.

Truly, once you read this book you will never look at American history in the same way!

A Note From The Author

Hello, this is Jack Rosewood. Thank you for reading Murder In Wisconsin. I hope you enjoyed the read of this chilling story. If you did, I'd appreciate if you would take a few moments to post a review on Amazon.

Thanks again for reading this book, make sure to follow me on Facebook at Jack Rosewood Author.

Best Regards
Jack Rosewood

Made in the USA
Monee, IL
12 April 2023